Standing on Holy Common Ground

AN AFRICENTRIC MINISTRY APPROACH TO
PROPHETIC COMMUNITY ENGAGEMENT

BY
LESTER AGYEI McCORN

Ernest J Gaithings

Keep the faith!
Ralph Nelson

Standing on *Holy* Common Ground

AN AFRICENTRIC MINISTRY APPROACH TO PROPHETIC COMMUNITY ENGAGEMENT

BY

LESTER AGYEI M^cCORN

MMGI BOOKS, CHICAGO, ILLINOIS

"*Standing on Holy Common Ground is an insightful reflection on how the modern-day church can fulfill its mission and purpose while holding fast to the prophetic tradition and principles in the African-American community. Lester A. McCorn identifies creative approaches to how the church can reach the communities in which they reside while making the Gospel relevant by using an Afrocentric approach to outreach and evangelism.*"
Rev. Delman Coates, Ph.D.,
Senior Pastor, Mt. Ennon Baptist Church, Clinton, Maryland

"*In this time of rapid crisis and mega change, the prophetic dimension of the Black Church tradition needs to formulate fresh expressions to serve this present age. Lester McCorn, a seasoned pastor- scholar, brings practical wisdom to the task of bridging liberation theology with church and community development. I highly commend* Standing on Holy Common Ground.*"
Rev. Jeffery L. Tribble, Sr., Ph.D.
Associate Professor of Ministry
Columbia Theological Seminary, Decatur, Georgia

"*Dr. Lester Agyei McCorn provides an inter-disciplinary approach to community empowerment that is practical and necessary. Utilizing an African-centered ethos grounds his research, making it indigenous to the church's congregants and the community's residents. Dr. McCorn builds a bridge to the future of the post-modern, post-civil rights urban metropolis. This is a much needed addition to scholarship about the Black Church and urban ministry. It is made more authoritative by the fact that the author is practicing what he is preaching in Baltimore.*"
Rev. S. Todd Yeary, Ph.D.
Douglas Memorial Community Church, Baltimore, Maryland

"*Dr. McCorn presents a clear and certain sound calling for a reconciled and restored relationship between the Black Church and the community it has historically served. The burden is justifiably placed upon the church. The inter-disciplinary engagement of black theology, pastoral care, biblical exegesis, cultural history, Christian ethics, and sociology serves to certify the scholarship. The "sermonic" interludes, references to the personal journeying, and the concluding modeling provides practical substance for the theoretical. The use of the Africentric lens and the prophetic perspective adds to the relevance and to the reliability of this much needed work. We are the richer for it!*"
Bishop Nathaniel Jarrett,
A.M.E. Zion Church (Retired)

"*Dr. McCorn makes us proud. His scholarship represents the hope needed for our progress. God has uniquely gifted Lester to bend his pastoral lens to common community issues. Through precise critical analysis, and methodological resolve,* Standing on Holy Common Ground *places this young social scientist soundly among his academic peers. Read then do.*"
Rev. Ivan Douglas Hicks, Ph.D.
Pastor, First Baptist Church North, Indianapolis, Indiana

"The African American Church historically existed right in the middle of African American life. Everything from educating our children to helping adults become job ready; the Church provided both leadership and common meeting ground to advance the African American culture. Much competes with that prophetic placement the church has historically held. Dr. McCorn, sternly and pastorally calls us to use that God empowered placement the church has in the lives of African American's to call us to a new community engagement. Some may ask, "Where have the prophets gone?" I know where one does his ministry work; it's in the city of Baltimore at the Pennsylvania Avenue A.M.E.Z Church. This is a must read!"

Dr. William H. Curtis,
Pastor, Mt. Ararat Baptist Church, Pittsburgh, PA and
Former President, Hampton Ministers Conference

"Dr. Lester McCorn's work in the African American church is lifelong, laudable, and liberating. As an extension of that work, he has penned this stalwart contribution to the church that intersects ecclesiology, anthropology, liberation theology, history, and black church studies. There is much to be appreciated about this volume. In only eight chapters Dr. McCorn captures the gestalt of Afrocentric renewal and prophetic engagement between the church and the community. With meticulous scholarship and readability, Dr. McCorn offers a narrative monograph that instructs and inspires readers. As a budding Afro-Ecclesiologist, with this text McCorn has become a significant dialogue partner in the larger conversation centered on the black church."

Bishop Johnathan E. Alvarado, D.Min.
Senior Pastor, Grace Church International, Atlanta, Georgia
Professor of Theology/Dean of the Chapel, Beulah Heights University, Atlanta, Georgia

"This work by Lester Agyei McCorn provides the framework to embrace the linkage between the foundational principles once associated from the inception of the Black Church and Africentric cultural values. This ministry model establishes a firmer foundation for renewing and rediscovering the empowerment measures of the inner workings between the pew and pulpit. Therefore, I whole heartedly endorse Standing on Holy Common Ground, which shall be an invaluable asset for years to come through this level of research and scholarship in the African American community. The Black Church shall be empowered to raise its collective voice as the sacred meets the secular together as one."

Dr. Willie A. Gholston II
Pastor, Bethel African Methodist Episcopal Church, Chicago, Illinois

"Standing on Holy Common Ground *is a must read for any congregation who is serious about making a difference in the world. Dr. McCorn has taken community development to the cutting edge."*

D. Darrell Griffin
Pastor Oakdale Covenant Church, Chicago, Illinois and
Author of *Navigating Pastoral Leadership*

"Dr. Lester McCorn may be a name which is new to some, but for those in the AME Zion tradition his name is synonymous with congregational revitalization and community transformation. For almost thirty years, Dr. McCorn has been so busy doing the work that he has had little time to reflect on and record what has informed his pastoral outlook and prophetic actions. In Standing on Holy Common Ground, he gives a glimpse of how he has managed to do what many aspire to do: bridge the ever widening gap between the traditional Black Church and the first generation of youth and young adults (in the Urban North East) who were not raised in nor influenced by the Black Church: Baby Busters and Millennialists. This is a must read for anyone who wants to get a better grip on how to make meaningful connections with that demographic without being perceived as dated, condescending, and inauthentic."

Rev. Anthony L. Trufant
Pastor, Emmanuel Baptist Church, Brooklyn, New York

"Standing on Holy Common Ground is a must read for pastors and para-church ministries because it stretches our theological parameters and propels us to not only minister in the confinements of extravagant edifices but to actualize our calling, as conduits of God, outside of the four walls of our sanctuary in order to offer an appropriate response to the plight of our communities. According to Lester Agyei McCorn, it is when our community becomes our sacred pulpit that social ministry and urban revitalization happens."

Dr. Darron McKinney
Pastor, Macedonia Baptist Church, Baltimore, Maryland

"Dr. Lester Agyei McCorn has written a must read book for every one concerned about the deliverance and development of the 21st Century Black Church and Community. Standing on Holy Common Ground is a spiritual and intellectual document that celebrates the strong roots of the empowering Black Faith Tradition while establishing a foundation for building strong 21st Century liberating relationships and institutions. Theologically rich, intellectually innovative, historically sound and creatively Christio-centric Standing on Holy Common Ground is a road map for those who want to make a difference and change the world for Christ!"

Dr. Frank Madison Reid III
Pastor, Bethel A.M.E. Church, Baltimore, Maryland

"Dr. Lester A. McCorn provides an insightful perspective on one of the most difficult challenges of Pastors of African American Churches, 'How to reconnect them to the African American community where they are domiciled?' With the precision of a scholar, researcher, and practical theologian he directs us to the nexus, 'The Holy Common Ground.' Read this book, learn from this book, and implement the ideas contained in this book and your ministry will be blessed and fruitful."

Dr. Alvin C. Hathaway
Pastor, Union Baptist Church, Baltimore, Maryland

"Dr. Lester Agyei McCorn has spent much time in scholarly research, as well pastoral ministry, assessing the condition of the Black Church. Standing on Holy Common Ground challenges the Black Church to return to the origin of its mission of building black communities through an Africentric biblical perspective. The black church must reclaim its own evangelical identity by reconnecting its work to the black communities who struggle to see the relevance of the black church. Dr. McCorn has laid the path for this to happen in this book."

Rt. Rev. Dr. C. Nathan Edwers
Presiding Prelate of Middle Atlantic Conference (NJ & NY)
Unified Free Will Churches

"The life and journey of Lester Agyei McCorn has clearly been guided by God's gracious hand and prepared him for the task he now has undertaken, to serve as scribe and scholar for the church and the culture, culminating in this salient work. His call and challenge demands of us more so that we may be worthy of Standing on Holy Common Ground. His work reminds us to abandon the self-serving purposes to which too much of modern ministry has fallen prey."

Dr. Kenneth Q. James
Pastor, Memorial A.M.E. Zion Church, Rochester, New York

"What Dr. Lester A. McCorn provides in Standing on Holy Common Ground is some keys that will aide us in addressing the disconnect, the brokenness and the spiritual decline that is often associated with the African American Church. In a profound, yet understandable manner, Dr. McCorn dissects and examines the layers of experiences and spiritual episodes within the African American church and community, from historical to present. Anyone who is serious about addressing present problems and preparing for the next generation as it relates to church and community cannot forfeit this tome. I am excited over this work that contributes to the effort that enhances church and community."

Dr. James L. Carter
Pastor, Ark Church, Baltimore, Maryland

"In an era marked by widespread division, distrust and disappointment, Dr. Lester Agyei McCorn's call for reconciliation and restoration via Africentric spirituality and values is a historically time tested means of community empowerment. The 21st century Black Church and Community will find in this scholarly work an inspiring light by which they may navigate through present difficult circumstances towards that 'Holy Common Ground' upon which a 'Beloved Community' may be built. Standing on Holy Common Ground: An Africentric Ministry Approach to Prophetic Community Engagement is a must read for all serious aspirants seeking to build bridges and help heal the hurts that hinder the advancement of God's Will for a better world."

Dr. Arnold Howard
Pastor, Enon Baptist Church, Baltimore, Maryland

Published by MMGI Books, Chicago, IL 60636
www.mmgibooks.com

Standing on Holy Common Ground:
AN AFRICENTRIC MINISTRY APPROACH TO PROPHETIC COMMUNITY ENGAGEMENT

Copyright © 2013 by Lester A. McCorn
All rights reserved.

No part of this publication may be reproduced, stored in a retrieval system, or transmitted in any form or by any means, electronic, mechanical, photocopying, recording, or otherwise, without the prior permission of the copyright owner, except for brief quotations included in a review of the book.

MMGI Books has made every effort to trace the ownership of quotes. In the event of a question arising from the use of a quote, we regret any error made and will be pleased to make the necessary corrections in future printings and editions of this book.

Bible quotations in this volume are from The Holy Bible, King James Version (KJV). Used by permission. All rights reserved. New International Version 1984 Holy Bible, New International Version®, NIV® Copyright © 1973, 1978, 1984 by Biblica, Inc.® Used by permission. All rights reserved worldwide.

Library of Congress Cataloging-in-Publication Data
Standing On Holy Common Ground: An Africentric Ministry Approach to Prophetic Community Engagement by Lester A. McCorn

    p. cm

ISBN 978-1-939774-00-2 (pbk. :alk. Paper)

Church Development. 2 Community Development. 3. Religious life. 4. Conduct of life. McCorn, Lester A.

Printed in the U.S.A.

TABLE OF CONTENTS

DEDICATION	2
ACKNOWLEDGEMENTS	3
EPIGRAPH	6
FOREWORD	7
INTRODUCTION: When We Remember Zion	9
CHAPTER ONE: The Road Less Traveled: A Spiritual and Intellectual Journey	17
CHAPTER TWO: Zion Stands with Hills Surrounded: A Black Church in the African American Community	23
CHAPTER THREE: Over in Zion: The African Church in America	31
CHAPTER FOUR: Repairing the Breach: The Black Church's Dual Role of Reconciliation and Restoration	45
CHAPTER FIVE: Blow the Trumpet in Zion: The Role of Black Theology	51
CHAPTER SIX: Marching to Zion: An Africentric Approach to Prophetic Engagement	59
CHAPTER SEVEN: Can the Bones Live?: A Biblical Vision for Restoration of the African American Community	79
CHAPTER EIGHT: The Beautiful City of Zion: A New Holy Common Ground	89
APPENDIX A	97
APPENDIX B	109
BIBLIOGRAPHY	113

DEDICATION

This book is dedicated to the A.M.E. Zion Church – The Freedom Church – and the Zion churches that have allowed me to practice prophetic ministry. I am grateful for the pastors who saved my life and shaped my being as a preacher of the gospel, Dr. William E. Kelly, Dr. W. Robert Johnson, III, Rev. Nathaniel K. Perry and Bishop Warren M. Brown.

I dedicate this book to the sainted memory of my mother, Bettyann L. McCorn-Coles, my grandmother, Henrietta C. McCorn and my first Sunday school teacher, Louise Bertha Baskerville.

I also dedicate this to the Reverend Dr. Gardner C. Taylor, the "Dean of Black Preachers," for his sterling example of excellence in preaching, prophetic leadership and ecumenical cooperation. I am honored to be associated with his legacy.

ACKNOWLEDGEMENTS

This book is the product of a village collaboration that spans time and space. I am indebted to the people of the Pennsylvania Avenue African Methodist Episcopal Zion Church of Baltimore, Maryland for their patience and support during the research and development of this meaningful project. I am especially indebted to Rose Jones, Rose Horton, Teresa Stephens, Wanda Best and Gordon Clark who have shared with me the labor of researching this topic.

The "Zion Church" is the last of many A.M.E. Zion congregations that I have been privileged to pastor. Each of the previous congregations, from the rural Hemphill and Bush Chapel churches in Georgia, to the urban ministries of St. Luke Christian in Dorchester (Boston), Varick Memorial in New Haven, Martin Temple in Chicago and Faith in Atlanta, have given me a safe place to serve and grow into the life's mission to which God has called me. It all began in a modest church in Worcester, Massachusetts known as Belmont Street A.M.E. Zion Church. They nurtured me, loved me and helped prepare me for a pastorate of prophetic proclamation.

Moreover, I am grateful that I was able to recently take a trip up the East Coast with members of the Zion Church of Baltimore to Belmont Church in Worcester. Belmont Church sent me to Morehouse College on "a wing and a prayer." They have taught me to say, "I have a dream" and provided me with the opportunity to follow in Dr. King's footsteps. Hence, I now have the opportunity to help others who have come from the same impoverished background to dream of a Beloved Community in which they have significant roles and responsibilities.

I also acknowledge the plethora of professors who have inspired and shaped my thinking about ministry from an Africentric perspective. I was introduced to Black theology from a practical perspective in the basement of Belmont Street Church by teachers who taught me what the African in A.M.E. Zion meant. This was affirmed and expanded by my introduction to Pan-

Africanism in the Martin Luther King, Jr. Chapel at Morehouse College. It was Dean Lawrence Edward Carter who became my first intellectual mentor. He brought together for me the social justice imperatives preached by Dr. King with the rich, cultural heritage of the African Diaspora. He supported me during my difficult periods as a poor student at Morehouse. On several occasions he gave me a platform to find my voice. He allowed me to have my African naming ceremony in King Chapel on a Sunday morning. The ritual was performed by another important figure in my spiritual and intellectual formation, Dr. Ndugu G.B. T'Ofori-Atta. Dr. "T", who was the first mystical sage I had ever met, was the pastor of my adopted church in Atlanta, Shaw Temple A.M.E. Zion Church, and a professor at the Interdenominational Theological Center. I was honored to be one of his mentees and, later on, his pastor.

Other people have also played significant roles in my intellectual evolution. I was blessed to have several prophetic professors who embodied the Africentric ethic of community: Lawrence E. Carter and Aaron L. Parker of Morehouse College, the late Anthony Campbell of Boston University School of Theology, the late Edwin Edmonds of Southern Connecticut State University, Gilbert Bond at Yale University Divinity School, JoAnne Marie Terrell, Julia Speller and Lee Butler of Chicago Theological Seminary, Larry Murphy, Henry Young and Jeffery Tribble of Garrett-Evangelical Seminary, David Daniels of McCormick Theological Seminary and Dwight Hopkins of University of Chicago Divinity School.

I am proud to be a Gardner C. Taylor Fellow of United Theological Seminary. I was blessed to be a part of a praxis community of friends and colleagues committed to helping the Church continue to be faithful to its mission. We were led by two preacher-prophets who ably represent the spirit of Dr. Taylor, the dean of Black Preachers. The powerful father-son team of Drs. H. Beecher Hicks and Ivan Douglas Hicks were valued mentors and interlocutors. The former is one of the greatest preachers of his generation and the latter is destined to follow suit.

I want to thank my long-time friend and Morehouse brother, Dr. Otis Moss III, for writing the foreword to this volume. Dr. Moss leads one of the best examples of an Africentric, prophetic ministry in the country, the Trinity United Church of Christ of Chicago. He personally embodies the great prophetic leadership tradition, while his congregation has made a major impact across the African diaspora, beginning in its South Side Chicago neighborhood. Trinity and Pastor Moss are surely "standing on holy common ground."

I acknowledge the support of my cohort of advisors and trusted colleagues, Dr. Alvin Hathaway, Dr. S. Todd Yeary, and Dr. Guy Williams, Sr. They have provided invaluable guidance and inspiration at several phases of my intellectual growth.

Finally, I do not exaggerate when I say that I am nothing without the family with which God has blessed me. I am indebted to my loving and faithful wife, Charlene Mundy McCorn. She has given me the inspiration and support necessary to fulfill my calling as a "doctor of the church." She has been my constant companion and ministry partner at for twenty years and our children, William Elijah, Maliaka, and John-Charles give me a reason every day to do my best to make this world a better place for them and their children. I love them profoundly and am most appreciative of being a recipient of their unconditional love. I thank them for being patient and understanding when daddy had to spend countless hours in the study instead of spending desired time with them. Hopefully, this book will prove that their sacrifice was worthwhile.

EPIGRAPH

We are Standing on Holy Ground

We are standing on holy ground

And I know that there are angels all around

Let us praise Jesus now

We are standing in His presence

On holy ground.

Geron Davis, *We are Standing on Holy Ground*

FOREWORD

Like Jazz, worship in the Black community has always been dynamic and fluid. Our historical struggles, socio-economic status and theological reflection are woven into the fabric of Black religious experience. The Black church, according to scholar Melville Herskovitz, is a matrix of African rituals, beliefs, and values infused with the unique American experience of slavery and liberation ethic of the Gospel. The Church has been and is a sacred space of creative freedom and imagination. The Black Church historically has been the place where men and women of color could be full human beings outside the oppressive watchful eye of "slave masters."

The majority of Black institutions find their genesis in the womb of the church. Historically black colleges, black insurance companies, the civil rights movement, civic organizations and labor unions were born within the walls of the church. The Black Church is critical to our understanding of black cultural productions such as blues, jazz, spirituals, linguistic nuances and political ideologies of the black community. This "invisible institution" or faith community developed on plantations, near streams and around hidden fields is the place where people of African descent reflected theologically on their collective experience of pain in America. The earliest independent Black churches Silver Bluff Baptist in Silver Bluff, South Carolina, African Baptist of Mecklenburg, Virginia, and First African in Savannah, Georgia all were birthed within the matrix African religious values and western constructs of class. What must be noted about the black church birthed in the antebellum south is the move from invisible to a visible institution. The Black church was prone to institutionalize southern social forces, which would create acceptance and rejection of different African motifs inherit in Black expression. In other words we went from African-centered to Euro-centric as pressure from the wider society sought to erase our Africanity.

Most scholars agree, during the 1700's to 1800, many Black churches exemplified a worship style, which was connected to their West African roots. African chants, metered music, Spirituals, and praise hymns were the norm. Call and response worship services sprinkled with spirit possession called "catching the Holy Ghost" or "getting happy" was normative. The era of reconstruction brought a change in the Black church. As men and women found a degree of mobility in the segregated south, the growing black middle class rejected "African" influenced modes of worship. The call and response of spirituals, African chants and the new "middle class" looked down upon the ring shouts of the earlier generation. The name "African" during this period was dropped from use. With the increasing stratification between rural and urban worshippers, which was intensified by the culture of classism, worship changed rapidly in the Black church. Churches now defined themselves not only by denomination, but also by class, and in some cases, color. "Educated" people who were trained from the euro-centric perspective populated many middle class churches, especially those from predominantly white denominations. European anthems, hymns and liturgy were appealing to the congregants. The modes of worship associated with Africa developed in the fields of the south were rejected by the sons and daughters of Africa seeking acceptance from the wider society. This is the beginning of what many of us call the "traditional church."

It is in this context Pastor Lester McCorn seeks to bridge the gap created by the post emancipation church. Pastor McCorn has distinguished himself as one this generation's greatest prophetic voices deeply committed to reclaiming our Africanity and Christianity. As a pastor in Chicago, Atlanta and Baltimore he has led congregations to a closer walk with Christ and deeper understanding of their heritage. His messages blend thoughtful exegesis, prophetic witness and authentic Africanized expression. It is tragic many ministers have rejected their history and preach a westernized Jesus constructed post enlightenment by theologians seeking to maintain European hegemony. I am delighted to call Pastor McCorn friend and over the years witness his stellar leadership. I know the book you hold will enlighten, challenge and bless your life as you "Stand On Holy Common Ground" and reclaim what enslavers sought to erase and inept theologians tried to deny.

Reverend Dr. Otis Moss III

INTRODUCTION
WHEN WE REMEMBERED ZION

By the rivers of Babylon, there we sat down.
Yea, we wept when we remembered Zion.
Psalm 137:1

The multi-layered narrative history of the African American community, especially in urban centers, has been fraught with ambiguity and incongruity, shame and success, tragedy and triumph. It would appear as nothing less than miraculous that many generations of African Americans since slavery and Jim Crow segregation have survived and even thrived in a nation where they were perniciously and systemically dehumanized and demoralized by the state-sanctioned policies and practices of white supremacy and racism.[1] During the twentieth century American metropolises emerged as the new "Promised Land" for African Americans looking for equality, economic opportunity and "the American Dream." Along with the upward climb came multiple stressors affecting several social institutions, government, financial, political and familial. The proverbial pie had to be cut into more pieces, usually unequal, with the largest pieces going to the most powerful segments of society. Most African American families were kept intact by amazing informal and formal networks of kinship and support. At the heart of those networks has been the Black Church, which has held an indisputable and indispensable position in the historical, cultural, social and political milieu of the American city.[2]

As one of the main facilitators of the acculturation of Black family life in urban centers, the Black Church has performed several meaningful and essential roles. The antecedents of the Black Church and African American

---
1   See James Cone's *The Cross and the Lynching Tree* in which he shares his perspectives about the strategies that blacks used as a means of survival during this period in American history. Cone, *The Cross and the Lynching Tree* (NY: Orbis Books, 2011).
2   The Black Church is not a monolithic institution but is comprised of a variety of religious denominations. However, for the sake for brevity I choose to use the term "Black Church" as a socio-theological referent for those black religious protestant institutions that originated from the Black African- American religious experience.

community are firmly rooted in the African religious and cultural traditions which were born in Africa and took on new life in America. However, the last forty years has seen a dramatic shift in the role of the Black Church as an advocate and facilitator of African American social progress and stability, notwithstanding the phenomenon of the Black mega church, which in many cases is conservatively evangelical and conspicuously muted when it comes to African American issues.

The African American community has suffered much calamity in the Post-Civil Rights era. A marked decline in viability and cohesion can be traced to the assassination of Dr. Martin Luther King Jr. in 1968 and the subsequent riots that occurred in several U.S. cities. The steady disinvestment in the inner city robbed Black communities of valuable assets, institutions, and stable families. Several attendant factors affected the social and ethical composition of the Black Church. Dr. H. Beecher Hicks, the senior pastor of the prominent Metropolitan Baptist Church of Washington, D.C. talks about the dramatic change in the context of the Black Church. He evinces that the church is no longer concerned with issues of social justice despite the fact that the neighborhoods in which these churches are located are plagued with pathologies such as unemployment, under-employment, homelessness, illnesses, crack and cocaine use, and crime. According to Dr. Hicks, "The Church is losing its posture of influence and is no longer the voice of social justice or the conscience that promotes personal piety or spiritual maturity." Hicks believe that it is because of these pathologies that many have turned from the church, finding it irrelevant. He notes:

> Throughout the nation the African American Church is often faced with an unveiled hostility on the part of those who seek to wrest control of the community from its historic residents. As diversity comes to the inner city there has also come a new element of racial tension and a sense that institutions (particularly those that occupy a large space and are not on the tax rolls) are no longer desirable. In a word, the church that was once "in," a wanted and needed fixture of the community, is on the verge of being "out," forced to find suitable space in a suburban communities that are also beginning to demonstrate their own brand of hostility to religious institutions and other similar charitable and non-profit organizations.[3]

---

3   H. Beecher Hicks, Jr., Lecture presented to the Gardner C. Taylor Doctor of Ministry Scholars at United Theological Seminary, Dayton, Ohio, August 18, 2010.

The African American community has long relied on the Black Church as an agent and advocate of stability within a hostile society. Currently, however, there appears to be a lack of a concrete strategy of action from the church because of a perceived lack of information, interest, and involvement. Some have concluded that there is a growing schism between the faith community and the wider Black community. The Black Church can be accused of a "benign neglect" of the very communities in which most of them were birthed and belong. Fortunately, however, a key for renaissance can be found in a recovery of an Africentric communal ethos which involves re-establishing a partnership to revitalize and mobilize the church and the community by: sharing our common story, as an African-centered ethic, through the narratives of the residents and congregants; building consensus around our common goals (African "communalism"); and building common wealth (the African/Kwanzaa principle of Ujamaa) by sharing, developing and increasing our common assets.

Much of the resources and strategies of pastoral care has already been utilized in seeking to bridge and heal the emerging rupture between the Black Church and the African American community. However, by utilizing the methods of liberation theology and Christian community development, a praxis model has been developed to engage the church in liberating conversations that will lead to reconciliation and restoration. The foundation of this dialogue has been a spiritually grounded, African-centered worldview of the global community through the lens of the village community, which is to be valued, celebrated, protected and promoted.

Robert Michael Franklin, President emeritus of Morehouse College in Atlanta and author of *Crisis in the Village: Restoring Hope in African American Communities* points to the lack of attention by inner city congregations to the glaring problems of poverty, crime and misery. The Church has the capacity to do prophetic ministry in the midst of "missed opportunities."[4] He cites a 2003 report by R. Drew Smith, "Beyond the Boundaries: Low Income Residents, Faith Based Organizations and Neighborhood Coalition Building" which arrives at the following conclusions:

---

4 Robert M. Franklin, *Crisis in the Village: Restoring Hope in African American Communities* (Minneapolis: Fortress Press, 2007), 125.

- Two-thirds of the housing complex residents surveyed report having little or no contact with faith-based organizations in the previous year;
- Many congregations report having programs of potential value to neighborhood residents but indicate that church members take advantage of these programs more frequently than non-members; and,
- Roughly two-thirds of the congregations report that most of their members live more than one mile from their place of worship.[5]

One of the keys to restoring African American communities is an indigenous cultural and spiritual reconnection with the Black Church, and vice versa. In order for the connection to be authentic, it has to be more than transactional – political or economic. The connection has to be anchored in the recovery of a "holy common ground." At the center of this "holy common ground" is a truly African spiritual ethos. While many churches have made the overt attempt to infuse Africentrism, most have been drawn to the current evangelical trends that tend to "de-culturalize" and "de-colorize" the Gospel.[6] There appears to be a direct correlation between racial/social integration and the "de-radicalization" of the Black Church, which Gayraud Wilmore refers to as "the process of lessening social and political advocacy of Black ministers and churches in urban areas."[7] The diminishing concern for liberation and social change is a result of the increasing conservatism of the modern evangelical movement adopted by many Black churches. Many Black Churches have eliminated overtly African or African-American symbols, themes, language or images in the interest of becoming non-racial, post-racial or multi-cultural. Theologian James Cone argues that black churches lack a critical black theology and this leaves them vulnerable to the ideology and theology of white, evangelical churches. In *For My People: Black Theology and the Black Church* he contends:

> Without a clearly articulated theological position in creeds and theological text books, black preachers and their members have nowhere else to turn for theological knowledge and spiritual renewal except conservative,

---

[5] R. Drew Smith for the Leadership Center at Morehouse College, "Beyond the Boundaries: Low Income Residents, Faith Based Organizations and Neighborhood Coalition Building," Annie E. Casey Foundation Report (November 2003), 2. Available in PDF format at http://www.aecf.org.

[6] The term 'Africentricism,' which was first expounded on by Molefi Kete Asante, will be used interchangeably with the word Afrocentrism.

[7] Gayraud Wilmore, *Black Religion and Black Radicalism* (NY: Orbis Books, 2000).

white, evangelical churches. Of course, some black preachers and lay persons can and do transcend white theology and spirituality, but unfortunately, most do not know how to distinguish between black faith and white religion. And with the appearance of electronic church (on radio and television), black Christians are being lured from their spiritual heritage in black churches to the false gods of the Jerry Farwell's of this world. Without a critical black theology...black preachers are left with the option of simply imitating the false gods of the electronic church in order to keep their congregations from deserting the 11:00 a.m. service and other activities of their churches.[8]

The Black Church needs a spiritual and ideological and theological grounding that is true to its African roots. However, praxis, the practical application of theory in a reflexive-active interchange, is most important for the survival and liberation of African American communities. The early beginnings of the Black Church were explicitly African-centered as well as *Christocentric*. In *Africentric Christianity: A Theological Appraisal for Ministry,* J. Deotis Roberts explores the meaning of "Africentric Christianity." Deotis argues:

Africentrism is more than wearing African garments or dancing to percussive African music. It involves more than a cultural revival. It requires a new perspective of life, a cultural conversion. It leads to a new life view and worldview for African peoples. Africentrism builds upon the self-respect and empowerment aspects of the black consciousness-black power movement, the emphasis on blackness that gave rise to black studies and black theology. Africentric leaders give due credit to the contributions of persons such as Martin Luther King, Jr. and Malcolm X. Unlike the black power movement, Africentrism seeks to reinterpret our history and reconstruct our culture. It does not rest with slavery or with our ancestry in West Africa; it takes us back to classical African history in Ethiopia and especially Egypt.[9]

How does the Black Church recover its primary cultural and spiritual resource? How does she reconcile her strained and sometimes estranged relationship with increasingly secular African American neighborhoods?

---
8   James Cone, *For My People: Black Theology and the Black Church* (NY: Orbis Books, 2000), 120.
9   J. Deotis Roberts, *Africentric Christianity: A Theological Appraisal for Ministry* (Valley Forge: Judson Press, 2000), vii-viii.

How does she lead the restoration of dispirited, depleted, disenfranchised and disinvested urban communities? The answer can be found in the many successful models of responsible congregations that have become cultural and spiritual reservoirs of empowerment, advocating and partnering with communities to create an oasis in the middle of urban deserts of blight and depravity. Building on those examples, this book presents a praxis model that can be used by congregations to raise their collective consciousness and engage in practical methods of community transformation. Some churches that are already transforming communities through community development initiatives include: Greater Allen A.M.E. Cathedral of Jamaica-Queens, New York, Trinity United Church of Christ of Chicago, Illinois, St. Paul Community Baptist Church of Brooklyn, New York, Bridge Street A.M.E. Church of Brooklyn, New York, First A.M.E. Church of Los Angeles, California, and West Angeles Church of God in Christ of Los Angeles, California and others.[10]

My purpose for writing this book is to address the ongoing disconnect between the Black Church and the African American community, especially as it relates to neighborhood deterioration which adversely affects both institutions. The context for exploring this focus has been the Pennsylvania Avenue A.M.E. Zion Church in the Upton Community of West Baltimore, a "commuter-congregation." In understanding the need for communal relationships as it relates to the book's focus, one of my goals is to educate congregants to partner with community residents and institutions to develop common assets. The outcome embraces an Africentric understanding of community that compels the church to partner with its neighbors.

In Chapter One, I will recount my spiritual journey, allowing the reader insight into the experience of a young boy born to a single mother in the urban ghetto into ministry of social justice and community leadership. In this chapter, the intersection of my former and current contexts will be illuminated to demonstrate how God calls, equips, and sends willing servants from

---

10 Anthony Pinn describes the work of churches involved in community development. He notes, "From the Great Migration to the present the urbanization of black Americans has had benefits, but it also resulted in economic hardships expressed in part through substandard housing. Local churches, recognizing this dilemma, initiated subsidized housing. An example is the Nehemiah Homes Project (of the East Brooklyn Congregations—EBC), developed by fifty congregations in East Brooklyn during the early 1980s and chaired by (then pastor) Rev. Johnny Ray Youngblood of Saint Paul Community Baptist Church. Like the biblical figure Nehemiah, who rebuilds Jerusalem after its destruction, this project is concerned with rebuilding black neighborhoods." Anthony B. Pinn, *The Black Church in the Post-Civil Rights Era* (NY: Orbis Books, 2002), 79-80.

disenfranchised communities to speak truth to power and power to the people by preaching an Africentric Gospel of responsibility to the least, the lost, and the last in American society.

Chapter Two will address the existing body of literature that speaks to the historical and contemporary actions of the Black Church as an agent of survival and liberation for African American people. This chapter will survey the rich resources of Black Theology, Black Pastoral Care, and church-based community development.

Chapter Three explores the historical, biblical and theological foundations of this topic while dialoguing with experts in the fields relevant to this subject. Findings from this foundational exploration will result in the affirmation of existing models of ministry and validate the author's presuppositions toward new paradigms and practices of encouraging congregations and communities into greater participation in community development.

Chapter Four describes the desired dual role of the Black Church for reconciliation and restoration. The chasm between the Black Church and the African American community parallels the gulf between Black theology and the Black Church. A plan to bridge the perceived separation is discussed through the heuristic device of the Holy Common Ground. The chapter surveys the scholarship in the field, especially the work of Carroll Watkins Ali in Womanist and Pastoral Care scholarship.

Chapter Five reflects on the role of Black Theology in challenging and cajoling the Black Church to be more responsible to its mission. At the center of its quest, Black Theology seeks to ensure a practical goal of liberation for the oppressed. The sources of Black Theology are discussed, both an African-centered perspective and African American cultural milieu, in terms of their value for community empowerment.

Chapter Six is focused on an intentional, Africentric ministry approach to prophetic engagement. This chapter explores the preeminent significance of African spirituality and cultural values in restoring the African American community. Attention is paid to an ethical commitment to African-centered values that promote and preserve communal life in the face of the threatening reality of social, racial and economic injustice.

Chapter Seven presents an Old Testament exegetical vision of restoration for the African American community. The chapter examines the familiar account of the prophet Ezekiel in the Valley of Dry Bones. It provides a metaphor for community transformation, with the collaborative work of God, leadership and a prophetic community.

Chapter Eight gives us a New Testament example of prophetic community which lives in radical opposition to a self-serving, competitive, capitalistic society. Living on Holy Common Ground gives us a compelling motivation for building the Beloved Community of which Dr. Martin Luther King preached. The completed work is before the 21st Century church in community.

CHAPTER ONE
THE ROAD LESS TRAVELED: A SPIRITUAL AND INTELLECTUAL JOURNEY

I shall be telling this with a sigh
Somewhere ages and ages hence:
Two roads diverged in a wood, and I,
I took the one less traveled by,
And that has made all the difference.
Robert Frost

My journey is a direct outgrowth of my upbringing as the oldest child of a poor, single mother in the housing projects of Worcester, Massachusetts. My spiritual journey has been arduous and protracted. Diametrically, it has alternated from adversity to advantage, from pain to promise, from abject poverty to absolute perseverance. I am the oldest child of a poor, single mother who was born in the housing projects of Worcester, Massachusetts. Like many African American children, I was profoundly influenced by my grandmother, Henrietta Truesdale McCorn. A short, quiet, nondescript divorcee, "Gramma" seemed to have been somewhat isolated from her family of origin. She left Camden, South Carolina in the 1930s to move to Worcester, Massachusetts, never to return, unlike her siblings who maintained a connection to the Southern homeland. Worcester was a medium sized industrial city. It was located in the center of the region and was second only to Boston in size among New England cities. The city's Black population was less than 5%. Although she had several sisters who settled in the Northeast United States with their husbands and children, my Gramma did not seem to have much interaction with them. By the time I was born in 1966, Gramma was already divorced (or estranged, as many Black couples did not go through the official legal proceedings to dissolve a marriage). The family seemed to have limited contact with her former husband, William "Bill" McCorn, although I remembered visiting him in his home in "the country" in Millbury, Massachusetts. My mother, Betty McCorn, continued the same pattern of isolating herself from the family. My earliest memories of my childhood included Gramma walking me to Edward Street Daycare Center. My mother and I lived with Gramma until I was about five in an apartment in the historic Black Laurel/Clayton neighborhood in Worcester. We were forced to move when the federal experiment of urban renewal came to the city, wiping out the only solidly Black community in the old New England industrial center, 40 miles west of Boston. It was my first of many experiences of displacement. During my teenage years, my mother would struggle to keep it altogether. Often there was more month than money. A pattern of instability soon disrupted our living situation. We were evicted from several apartments in a five year span.

Nevertheless, the two constants of my life were church and school. Both would become very important as my family life soon became unstable and unpredictable, but I gained a love for both in those earliest days of life. One of the first books I read was a book of children's prayers given to me by Gramma. I was learning to communicate with God as I learned to read.

Mrs. Holmes, my sixth grade teacher, was considered the best teacher at Belmont Street Community School. She was a short, white, feisty, social activist and a fierce lover of children. She shared with her children a cosmopolitan dream of America as a place of equality and freedom for all people regardless of gender, color or creed. Even in that early post-civil rights era, she believed I represented hope for the future. At the same time I encountered Mrs. Holmes I had become a part of the dramatic ensembles put together by the Youth Director, Mrs. Louvenia Meeks, at Belmont Street Church. Sister Meeks had given me the leading role in a couple of black history programs. The most notable was the role of the Rev. Dr. Martin Luther King, Jr. I would frequently shed tears at the concluding crescendo of the speech, "Free at last, free at last. Thank God, almighty, we're free at last!" What moved me even more were the tears on other people's faces whenever I performed the speech.

At the age of 15 I began to feel some strange inner urgings while in church. I began to envision myself standing in the pulpit. I became enraptured with the preaching moment in church while my peers were playing and passing notes in worship service. I was developing a spiritual restlessness that evolved into dreams of being a preacher. My new pastor, Dr. W. Robert Johnson, also began to see and hear in my oratory an unusual giftedness for a young man and he encouraged me to pursue the ministry. Shortly after I turned 16, Dr.

Johnson scheduled me to give the Children's Day message. It would be my "trial sermon." I preached from the topic "Good Times," one of my favorite shows, because I saw the 1970s sitcom story of the Evans family in the projects of Chicago as my own story of growing up in poverty but still seeing "a bright side somewhere." The response to my preaching was tremendous. People congratulated, encouraged me, and wished me well.

Despite the encouragement I received in church, I was troubled with what I was experiencing at home. My mother was struggling with depression. She could not regain her stability or find a job. Because of my family's economic situation, I had started to work summer jobs when I was 13. At 15, I had gotten a job at Burger King that I was able to keep. Later, my pastor helped me get a job as a mail clerk at the regional Equifax office in downtown Worcester. Since my mother's welfare checks went 'mysteriously' missing, I became the sole breadwinner for my family. Family life again became tumultuous when we were again evicted. I became desperate and distraught and decided to call my pastor. Dr. Johnson responded to my distress by moving me into the parsonage. This experience changed the course of my life.

Dr. Johnson's tutelage helped to boost my self-esteem. I was elected president of my senior class and my grades improved dramatically. After inquiring about colleges, I was led to apply to a small historically black college in Atlanta that happened to be the alma mater of my hero, Rev. Dr. Martin Luther King, Jr. I was accepted, along with my friend and high school classmate, Chris Saunders. It was the beginning of the journey that altered my life forever. The slogan on the literature I received from the school said, "Be somebody. Be a Morehouse Man." I was determined to be somebody.

At Morehouse I met the man that would become my intellectual mentor, the Dean of the King Chapel, Dr. Lawrence E. Carter. Dean Carter was the "pastor" of the Morehouse Men. Upon meeting me, Dean Carter asked about my denominational affiliation, and when I told him, Dean Carter responded that he thought it was commendable that the A.M.E. Zion Church had kept the "African" in its name. I knew that Zion had deliberately chosen the African designation, but I had taken it for granted. That fall Dean Carter hosted the Nile Valley Conference, a historic, international event at King Chapel. It attracted Pan-African scholars and other intellectuals and activists from all over the world. The chief presenter was Dr. Cheikh Anta Diop, the renowned African historian. Other presenters included Ivan Van Sertima and Asa Hilliard. This conference forever shaped my thinking as an African in America and as an African American Christian minister. It was a watershed moment that began to bring together for me the meanings of faith and life, religion and politics, history and culture.

One of the participants of the Conference was Dr. Ndugu G.B. T'Ofori-Atta, formerly George B. Thomas, the pastor of Shaw Temple A.M.E. Zion Church in Atlanta and professor at I.T.C. Dr. T'Ofori-Atta became my spiritual mentor as pastor and Presiding Elder. He was fondly known as "Dr. T." Dr. T. helped me during my spiritual transformation at Morehouse. He led me in choosing a middle name that would be reflective of my African heritage and my sense of spiritual identity, a self-fulfilling prophecy. After doing research, the name *Agyei* was chosen. From the Akan tribe of Ghana, my new name meant "messenger of God." On my 23rd birthday, Dean Carter allowed me and Dr. "T" to have an African naming ceremony in the Martin Luther King Chapel. It was also Easter Sunday- the day of Resurrection.

A few weeks after my epiphany, I was assigned to the Bush Chapel A.M.E. Zion Church in Winder, Georgia, one of the stronger churches of the Georgia Conference. At 24 years old, I had become a community leader in Winder when a racially-charged issue occurred and a mass meeting, which I chaired, was organized to discuss what actions to take. The Barrow County Sheriff had been accused of police brutality, racial and sexual harassment and abuse. He was quoted as saying to a white woman who had filed a claim of abuse, "You should be thankful you were white and not a nigger or I would have killed you." The NAACP called a meeting and the president asked me to chair it. I was not totally surprised because I felt it was my calling as a socially-conscious minister and a Morehouse Man to lead during this kind of crisis. Barrow County had a legacy of racial hostility and inequality, and few Blacks had stood up and done something about it.

During this process, the course on "Community Organizing" which I had taken at Spelman College was relevant as I had to use the principles and practices I had learned then to navigate in this context. I also prepared for the mass meeting by reading a section in Taylor Branch's Pulitzer-Prize winning novel about the Civil Rights Movement's early years, *Parting the Waters*. I had read that Dr. King also prayed about what to say at the first meeting of what would be the Montgomery Improvement Association. He had started the meeting by speaking in measured tones, "We are here this evening – for serious business. We are here in a general sense, because first and foremost – we are American citizens – and we are determined to apply our citizenship – to the fullness of its means."[11] I imitated Dr. King's approach and began the meeting the same way. What was astonishing is that the County Sheriff came to the meeting. I felt the spirit of Dr. King rising within me as it had done when I was a 12 year old boy reciting his famous speech. I turned to the sheriff during his opening remarks and told him that we were demanding an apology and the immediate hiring of African American deputies in his office. If the sheriff did not comply with our demands, we would insist that he resign. For me, this was a "God moment." I felt that it was so much bigger than me at that moment in time. A new organization was formed – Citizens United to Rescue Barrow (CURB) – and Lester was elected its president. The organization won major victories when the sheriff agreed to recruit and hire more African Americans and the largest local bank agreed to recruit and hire African American tellers who would be allowed to be in line for management positions. I was beginning to grow into what would be my life's calling.

Several months later I began a new chapter in my life when I accepted an appointment to St. Luke Christian A.M.E. Zion Church in Boston (Dorchester), Massachusetts. It was a return home because I knew many of the members of this church from my childhood. During this time I also asked the love of my life, Charlene Mundy, to marry me and she accepted. My First Lady moved to Boston to join me, working hard to revive a declining congregation. I also accepted a position as a Community Organizer of a new church-based community organization called Mattapan-Dorchester Churches in Action. It was a perfect merger of my calling to preach and to effect grassroots change in communities. In two years, the year grew from 20 members to 120 members. The MDCA worked hard in stemming the decline in neighborhood stability and the increase in drug and gang activity. The group successfully influenced the implementation of a drug-asset forfeiture law that gave profits from seized drug-related assets to distressed communities.

---

11 Taylor Branch, *Parting the Waters: America in the King Years 1954-63* (NY: Simon & Schuster, 1988), 138-39.

After a couple of years in Boston, I had the opportunity to serve urban congregations in New Haven, Connecticut, Chicago, Illinois and Atlanta, Georgia. There we established community development corporations, housing for young men and senior women and soup kitchens for the hungry and homeless. I experienced the challenges of doing inner-city ministry that attempted to meet the various needs of underserved communities, with meager resources. All of these experiences prepared me for the monumental assignment of leading an historic church in a declining urban center, Baltimore, Maryland.

I was re-energized by the ministry context of Pennsylvania Avenue Church. It is a vibrant congregation located in a bustling urban center. It was a tall order to fill because it was proud of its prominence within the denomination, having its last three pastors elected to the episcopacy. Much of its ministry was centered on the personality of its previous leader, Dr. Dennis V. Proctor, a gifted and popular preacher. I soon discovered the need to rebuild the church's administrative infrastructure and expand its impact in the surrounding community. I have no doubt that my journey from the projects to homelessness to pastor to community organizer to Christian community developer has equipped me to lead this church in a renaissance for the ministry and for the historic Upton neighborhood. [12]

---

12 Stephen C. Raser and Michael J.N. Dash, *The Mark of Zion: Congregational Life in Black Churches* (Cleveland, Ohio: Pilgrim Press, 2003), 64. I understand the mission of the church as one that is uniquely situated within a community from which and for which its ministry is responsible and relevant. Stephen Raser and Michael Dash in *The Mark of Zion: Congregational Life in Black Churches* believe every congregation is called to ethically respond to the needs of the community in which it is located and that congregations can empower communities by responding to the community's needs. According to Raser and Dash, "Congregations have the capacity to affect their context through the ways in which they organize themselves and engage their context. Conversely the environment in which they find themselves affects and shapes the lives of congregations. Contextually aware congregations:
- Have a healthy self-awareness and understanding of themselves;
- Seek to hold institutions in their contexts accountable for the welfare of all persons, particularly the poor and helpless and hopeless;
- Are committed to working with other churches, agencies, and interest groups that struggle for justice;
- Live the life of faith beyond the walls and in the world;
- Engage in analysis through reflection and action

CHAPTER TWO
ZION STANDS WITH HILLS SURROUNDED: THE PENNSYLVANIA AVENUE A.M.E. ZION CHURCH

Zion stands with hills surrounded, Zion kept by power divine
All her foes shall be confounded, though the world in arms combine
Happy Zion, what a favored lot is thine!
Happy Zion, what a favored lot is thine![13]
Hymn by Thomas Hastings

The historic Pennsylvania Avenue African Methodist Episcopal Zion Church, also known as Zion Church, is located in one of the most socio-economically challenged neighborhoods in the city of Baltimore, Maryland. Known as one of the most prominent congregations in the AME denomination, Pennsylvania Avenue Church was founded in the city of Baltimore, Maryland in 1841. The Church has gone through several name changes in its history, having been originally established as an independent Black Methodist congregation and later joining the African Methodist Episcopal Zion Church denomination and moving to Pennsylvania Avenue and the historic Upton neighborhood in 1904. The current facility, which houses a 900-seat sanctuary, administrative wing, multi-purpose hall, and several classrooms, was erected in 1977. The 1,800-member congregation is generationally-diverse, with many of the members having been a part of the Church family for 50-plus years. The church operates over 20 ministries. The Church's first non-profit corporation, Zion Outreach Services, sponsored the construction of the adjacent senior residences, Zion Towers, in 1978. Although the Church is nearly 170 years old, it has a somewhat contemporary "feel" to it. The worship experience is very lively, with a full music band, contemporary praise team, and dance ministry. The church has two worship services on Sunday, at 8 and 10 a.m.

---

13   A.M.E. Zion Hymnal, A.M.E. Zion Publishing House: Charlotte, North Carolina, 1996.

The Upton community in which the church is located is less than a mile west of downtown Baltimore, was once considered the Harlem of Maryland. It was the cultural and political hub of Black Baltimore. It is the home of Thurgood Marshall, the legendary first African American Supreme Court Justice. It is also the home of the first African American Congressman of Maryland, Parren Mitchell and the current Congressman Elijah Cummings. Upton is home to the first African American woman mayor of the city, Sheila Dixon, along with the second African American woman mayor, Stephanie Rawlings-Blake. Both women are members of churches in the Upton Community, and rose to the mayor's office after being the President of the City Council. The main thoroughfare of Upton, Pennsylvania Avenue was home to the most vibrant entertainment and cultural fare of the city. It once housed the famed Royal Theatre, which rivaled the historic Apollo Theatre of New York in the caliber of talent that played that venue and other famous places on "The Avenue," like the Club Casino, Ike Dixon's Comedy Club, Gamby's, and the Sphinx Club. These spots showcased the likes of Cab Calloway, Dizzy Gillespie, Duke Ellington, Billie Holiday, Dinah Washington, Redd Foxx, Slappy White and Pearl Bailey.[14] Many remember the glory days of the Avenue. However, Christina Royster-Hembry also notes that it was a strange creation of the racist climate of the Baltimore of the early- to mid-twentieth century:

> While the Avenue may have been the place to be back in the day, it prospered because it existed amid the segregation of Jim Crow-era America. Blacks couldn't go to the Hippodrome or to Baltimore Street for entertainment, and the theaters blacks could and did attend, such as the Royal, were often owned by whites. Yet, within this harsh, segregated world, Pennsylvania Avenue also served as a bittersweet point of pride—the only place in town one might see Hollywood-worthy black names on a marquee.[15]

It was during this "Renaissance" that the Pennsylvania Avenue Church saw its most dramatic growth, under the leadership of the Reverend George Marion Edwards, a beloved pastor that many of the Church's members fondly remember as the man who made the church a center of the community. During

---
14 Royster-Hembry, Christina, Baltimore City Paper, "Street of Dreams," February 2, 2005
15 Ibid.

the 1940s and 50s, the church had a pseudo-renaissance that paralleled the cultural and economic resurgence that the Upton community experienced. However, the next three decades saw the decline of businesses, owner-occupied dwellings, housing values, jobs, and two-parent households. It now has the lowest indices of social-economic health in the city of Baltimore. The Upton/West Baltimore neighborhood is the setting for the famed HBO-series "The Wire" with a tainted backdrop of crime, poverty, gang warfare, drug activity, and political and police corruption. Harold A. McDougall conducted a thorough study of the history of Black Baltimore. He spent a considerable amount of time exploring the West Baltimore neighborhoods of Upton, Sandtown and Druid Heights. McDougall reported:

> Blacks in Baltimore remember segregation as a cruel symbol of inequality, but they also remember it as a context for stable black vernacular neighborhoods, with a strong work ethic and closely networked local economies. While well-meaning middle-class black people mobilized, lobbied, and politicked, often, but not always, on behalf of the entire black community, they sometimes lost contact with low-income black people, and so lost sight of their needs and aspirations. The limited results of black electoral achievements demonstrate that formal political empowerment alone is unlikely to galvanize the black community's informal leaders to root progress and development deep into the underclass. The support networks that once were the greatest resource of vernacular West Baltimore must be recreated. A leadership approach that relies more on networking within the community, and less (or at least not exclusively) on "big bang" political and economic strategies, is needed to create more lasting improvement in the black community, and to include all of its members in the work of change as well as in the rewards of change.[16]

The church is situated in the middle of this neighborhood, which has gone through a major decline over the last forty years. The previous pastor of the Zion Church, Dr. Dennis V. Proctor, formed what was called Zion Development Corporation, Incorporated (ZDC). The ZDC operated an after school program and a computer program for children and senior adults. It had

---

[16] Harold A. McDougall, *Black Baltimore: A New Theory of Community*, (Philadelphia: Temple University Press, 1993), 113.

plans to build a community center, but the plans were delayed indefinitely when there was a change in the mayoral administration that was favorable to the pastor and the ZDC.

The Upton Planning Committee is the neighborhood association that represents the interest of the immediate community. The 2004 Upton Master Plan gives this ominous assessment of the neighborhood:

> In Upton, sixty percent of families with children under five years old are living in poverty. Children who are born into poverty are more likely to be poor as adults. Furthermore, living in a neighborhood where almost everyone else is also poor greatly increases an individual's likelihood of being poor as an adult. The reasons that neighborhood conditions have such a strong influence on individual success vary greatly, from a lack of positive role models to a lack of institutional support systems, but the relationship between neighborhood concentrations of poverty and the ability of an individual to achieve the American Dream is clear.[17]

Despite its many ministries, some members believe that the Church should become more involved in the community. In a survey conducted to get feedback from a core group of church members, some of them raised the issue of the perceived disconnect between the church and community. One person stated, "The church seems 'too guarded' and protected from the community." Another said that the relationship between the church and the community is divided mainly because of class differences. The Church is perceived as a middle-class congregation and the community is perceived as poor and working class. It was pointed out that historically the neighborhood was more middle class, with mostly homeowners and professionals. Another person said, "Many preachers are out of touch with the under-served population. It is important for ministers and churches to ask people what they feel they need rather than assume they know what's best for them." Most agreed that many churches were providing some programs for the community. A couple of churches were even mentioned for doing community development through housing and a head start center. All agreed that the church could and should do much more.

---

17   Upton Master Plan.

Members of the church expressed a deep concern for the state of the community, but they had not experienced a deliberate attempt by the church to connect the Bible and Christian faith with the mandate to transform the community. They had heard sermons and seen some programs that seemed to help people. But there was not a concerted effort to move the congregation into specific, concrete steps that led to comprehensive, grass roots, bottom-up, inclusive community development. One woman was very clear that it was her upbringing in the church and in a family of believers that led her to commit her life to making the community better. She personally became an activist and an advocate. She wanted her church to do the same. Another person said that her faith had motivated her to want to improve her neighborhood. Although she had written at least four resignation letters from her position on the board of the neighborhood association, her faith would not let her walk away.

The church had done some things in the past, but its recent involvement was less than impressive. The church had a community development corporation that ran some programs. There was an outreach center run from a row house that was donated to the church. Both were now defunct because of lack of interest and funding. The group thought these programs did some good. All agreed that social services were not enough. There needed to be some major initiative that emanated from the central mission of the church. It was said, "To fulfill its commandment the church should exist externally, outside the sanctuary. The church has to do more than back-to-school festivals, block parties and give-aways. We could use those funds to beautify the neighborhood." Another said, "We should not have to wait for a back-to-school festival to open our doors to our community. We need to evangelize more and make our voices heard." Members saw the church as a major player that could leverage tremendous resources for a comprehensive community development plan.

There is one major development initiative that could dramatically transform the landscape of the Upton community. The state of Maryland is slated to redevelop a new, massive State government office complex on 25 acres of land a few blocks East of Pennsylvania Avenue A.M.E. Zion Church. The State Center project is a $1.5 billion mixed use Transit Oriented Development (TOD) that includes: 1.2 million square feet of office/institutional space; 3,000 new housing units, and 500,000 square feet of retail/commercial space. While this looks like a favorable economic injection for a community that desperately needs it, it could also be a disastrous gentrification consequence that could displace hundreds of poor and working people, replacing them with middle- and upper-middle class people that have no affinity or affiliation with the history or the institutions of the neighborhood. Community leaders must guard against the kind of gentrification that has benefited more affluent citizens at the expense of its poorer citizens. Eugene Robinson describes the effects of gentrification on African American neighborhoods:

> Across the country, gentrification has turned dangerous, decrepit, close-in, once exclusively black neighborhoods into hip oases where the most outrageous crime is what coffee shops charge for a few drops of espresso mixed with some warm milk. This transformation is far from complete, it must be said, and there are cities where you could drive around for hours and decide that it hasn't made much of a dent at all. In Chicago, for example, vast sectors of the South Side are still unreconstructed ghetto, while in Baltimore whole neighborhoods of once-tidy row houses are abandoned, boarded up, and rotting away—the postapolyptic cityscape familiar to viewers of *The Wire*.[18]

Baltimore has been no stranger to the effects of gentrification as a consequence of major development projects that benefit middle and upper-middle whites. As McDougall observed about Baltimore's previous "big bang" project, the Inner Harbor:

> Despite an investment of over one billion dollars, Baltimore continued to lose middle-class citizens, industrial employment, and tax revenue, simultaneously experiencing growth in its low-income population. While tourists were flocking to the redeveloped Inner Harbor, Baltimore's young people were quietly flunking out of school. The black and poor people who occupied the downtown area before renewal were left worse off as their homes and communities were destroyed to make way for large transportation and infrastructure systems that were eventually underutilized by the businesses for which they were designed. Baltimore, the nation's eleventh-largest city, despite a resurgence in downtown economic activity, remains one of the nation's poorest cities, with

---
18   Eugene Robinson, *Disintegration: The Splintering of Black America*, New York: Doubleday, 2010, 122.

declining blue-collar employment, a faltering education system, among the highest teen-age pregnancy and infant mortality rates in the country, a deficient health care system for the poor, and a crisis in housing.[19]

As the pastor of Pennsylvania Avenue A.M.E. Zion Church, I have been a member of a coalition of proactive clergy, along with the pastors of four (4) other churches, who have advocated for an economic inclusion plan that guarantees jobs for community residents, with half of the construction jobs going to persons living within a mile radius of the State Center. The coalition, Community Churches for Community Development (CCCD), was instrumental in crafting the plan on behalf of the faith-based community in order to get the church more invested and engaged in a more comprehensive effort of community building, which includes housing, education, and economic development.

---

19   McDougall, 114.

CHAPTER THREE
OVER IN ZION:
THE AFRICAN CHURCH IN AMERICA

I got a new robe over in Zion and it's mine, mine, mine.
I got a new robe over in Zion and it's mine, mine, mine.
I got a new shout over in Zion and it's mine, mine, mine.
I got a new shout over in Zion and it's mine, mine, mine.
Traditional African American spiritual

In *The World and Africa*, by W.E.B. DuBois, Theodor Mommsen states:

It was through Africa that Christianity became the religion of the world. Tertullian and Cyprian were from Carthage; Arnobius from Sicca Veneria; Lactanius, and probably in like manner Minucius Felix, in spite of their Latin names, were natives of Africa, and not less so, Augustine. In Africa the Church found its most zealous confessors of the faith and its most gifted defenders.' In addition to Mommsen's statement, DuBois states, 'Origen, Athanasius, and Saint Cyril were from the Nile valley. At the head of the Catholic hierarchy at Rome, three popes were African by birth: Victor I (187-198), who defended the Roman date for Easter; Miltiades (311-314), who was pope when the Emperor entered Rome as a Christian; and Gelasius I (492-496), who defended the rights of the papacy against the state.'[20]

The Black Church is a unique, inimitable, and exceptional institution in American life. The roots of the Church run deep from Africa and represent the ferment of the Black freedom movement in the world. As the "Invisible Institution" it manifested a spirit of affirmation of humanity and resistance to horrific, systemic degradation. In time it became bureaucratic in form and function. However, the driving force of the Church was incontrovertibly spiritual. The Church became a powerful force in opposition against the

---

20 William Jacob Walls, *Reality of the Black Church: The African Methodist Episcopal Zion Church* (Charlotte: A.M.E. Zion Publishing House, 1974), 19.

demonic "principalities and powers" that sought to annihilate Black humanity and dignity. The spiritual identity of the Black Church is the most important element of its character and provides the potential for the recovery of a holistic Africentric ethos that can transform our communities. From its origins the Black Church maintained its cultural integrity. As Henry Mitchell states:

> The religious faith and practice of the masses of black Americans goes back even earlier than 1619; the continuum starts in Africa. In the words of Bruno Chenu, 'More than an imposition by the whites, it was the similarity between the Christian religion and their traditional religion that fostered the passage of the faith of the hated master. And African beliefs still lived beneath visible Christianity.'[21] Of course, this is contrary to the widely circulated assumption that Africans were largely stripped of their native culture and religion during or after their voyage to these shores. The truth is that there is much hard evidence proving that Africans retained a great deal of their original cultural heritage. This is especially true of religion, which was much harder to stamp out than visible behaviors such as styles of manual labor. The long-handled hoe of the colonies may have won out over the back-straining short-handled hoe of Africa, but the tenacity of the communally embraced traditional belief system was far greater. It was the people's psychic survival kit.[22]

Be that as it may, the modern Black Church, nevertheless, had to contend with its conflicted cultural identity in America, in what W.E.B. DuBois referred to as the "double-consciousness" of the Black psyche:

> The Negro is a sort of seventh son, born with a veil, and gifted with second-sight in this American world – a world which yields him no true self-consciousness, but only lets him see himself through the revelation of the other world. It is a peculiar sensation, this double-consciousness, this sense of always looking at one's self through the eyes of others, of measuring one's soul by the tape of a world that looks on in amused contempt and pity. One ever feels his twoness –an American, a Negro; two souls, two thoughts, two un-reconciled strivings; two warring ideals

---

21 Bruno Chenu, *The Trouble I've Seen* (Valley Forge: Judson Press, 2003), 48-49.
22 Henry H. Mitchell, *Black Church Beginnings: The Long Hidden Realities of the First Years* (Grand Rapids, Michigan: William B. Eerdmans Publishing Company), 2004, xv.

in one dark body, whose dogged strength alone keeps it from being torn asunder.[23]

However, the early Black Church helped to militate against this "double-consciousness" and give African Americans an authentic and holistic sense of self-respect, grounded in the biblical and theological reality of divine personhood.

The African Methodist Episcopal Zion Church, one of the first Black denominations, was formed in the crucible of harsh slavery and *de jure* segregation. Worshipping as inferior congregants in predominantly white churches did not sit well with Blacks who knew this contradiction was not biblically or theologically correct. In the heart of one of the emerging metropolises of America, Blacks decided to protest against the religious bigotry they were experiencing in the John Street Methodist Episcopal Church of New York City. They were loyal to the polity and practices of their Methodist identity. However, they chose to establish their own legitimate and authentic expression of the Christian religion. Mitchell further notes:

> In 1796, the black Methodists of New York City first met, with the permission and good wishes of Bishop Francis Asbury, who allowed them to 'hold such meetings in the intervals of the regular preaching hours of the white church.' Asbury was not always on hand, however, and the white Methodists of the John Street Church later engaged in the same kinds of subterfuge as the whites of St. George's in Philadelphia to maintain control of black church properties and church life. Notwithstanding delays due to fears because of the Gabriel Prosser revolt in Virginia as well as to internal problems, Zion sprang free with the formation of their own corporation on February 16, 1801, choosing the name of African Methodist Episcopal Zion Church. April 8 of the same year they managed to get title to some land. In 1806, Asbury ordained three deacons, including James Varick, who later became the first A.M.E. Zion bishop.[24]

The A.M.E. Zion Church became known as the "Freedom Church" because of its early embrace of its African identity in its name and its commitment

---
[23] W.E.B. DuBois, *The Souls of Black Folk* (New York: Bantam Books), 3.
[24] Mitchell, *Black Church Beginnings*, 69.

to the abolitionist and freedom struggle. The early adherents and leaders of the Church helped to give the Church its freedom identity: Sojourner Truth, Frederick Douglass, Harriet Tubman, Jermain Loguen, and Alexander Walters. Historian David Bradley relates that the AME Zion church appeared to be at the forefront in the era for the struggle for freedom because so many advocates of liberation came out of this denomination. He states:

> ...When Mother Zion (in New York City) was established, several of her leaders were individuals who owed their freedom to the Methodist Church and naturally that spirit of freedom became a fundamental part of the new organization.
>
> As one turns again to the lives of these Negro (sic) men and women it is not just a matter of chance that they belonged to the A.M.E. Zion Church. Once free, it was well known that this new church of freedom would leave no stone unturned in behalf of the new man. So all along the Mason and Dixon line, and farther west, in Ohio and Indiana, Zion Church men and their friends became beacon points of hope to the escaped slave, and no doubt out of gratitude and faith, they, likewise, became Zion members.[25]

Furthermore, the Black Church has historically held a predominant role for the Black community. It was part social agency, educational institution, mutual aid society, and political advocacy organization. Lewis Baldwin charts this role using famed historian Carter G. Woodson's term, "all-comprehending institution."[26] According to Baldwin, the Black Church did not view spirituality and socio-political involvement as mutually exclusive, but the Church while emphasizing spirituality became an agency of empowerment for Blacks. He reveals:

> ...The church had to move beyond the strictly *spiritual* and *ecclesiastical* to promote positive change in vital areas of life—social, political, economic, intellectual, and otherwise. This became all the more important for Africans in eighteenth- and nineteenth-century America, many of whom claimed the church as the only visible institution that they owned and controlled on a wide

---

25 David H. Bradley, *A History of the African Methodist Episcopal Zion Church* (Nashville: The Parthenon Press, 1956), 107-108.
26 Lewis V. Baldwin, "Revisiting the 'All-Comprehending Institution': Historical Reflections on the Public Roles of Black Churches," in R. Drew Smith, ed. *A New Day Begun: African American Churches and Civic Culture in Post-Civil Rights America* (Durham: Duke University Press, 2003), 15.

scale. This is what Carter G. Woodson had in mind when referring to the black church as an 'all-comprehending institution.'

...This politico-prophetic role that these churches would consistently assume in public affairs had become clear by the early 1800s, as they pointed to the paradox of a new nation born in freedom while more than 700,000 Africans languished in bondage. [27]

Baldwin also points to the "politico-prophetic role" of churches such as Richard Allen's African Methodist Episcopal Church (AME), James Varick's African Methodist Episcopal Zion Church (AMEZ), Peter Spencer's African Union Church, Thomas Paul's African Baptist Church, and other Black churches that were "forced into the public arena by the very nature of the black condition, and their tendency to combine a strong African consciousness and spirituality with an emphasis on racial advancement proved that there were centrifugal forces at work inside them." [28]

One of the key roles assumed by the early Black Church, which persisted for many decades, was that of economic empowerment. The Church was the sole institution owned by the African American community, and, as such, wielded a modicum of economic agency for the community. Lincoln and Mamiya explain that while the Black Church has "taken part in the financial and economic transactions of the larger society," it is the most economically independent institution in Black society that "does not depend on white trustees to raise funds" or on "white patronage to pay its pastor or erect its buildings." [29]

Church leaders understood that one of their best weapons against the pernicious effects of racism was harnessing financial power. Baldwin observes:

> The pervasiveness of racism led black church leaders to conclude that economic power was perhaps the most significant ingredient in their people's efforts to establish themselves as a force in both their own communities and in the society as a whole. This is why economic values, along with the virtues of education, were highlighted even in the books of doctrine and discipline put forth by African Methodists. In conformity with the Protestant work ethic, black churchpersons were taught to be

---

27　Ibid., 16.
28　Ibid., 15.
29　C. Eric Lincoln and Lawrence H. Mamiya, *The Black Church in the African American Experience* (Durham, North Carolina: Duke University Press, 1990), 241.

industrious, to avoid dealing in lotteries, to be prompt in paying debts, to be saving in their means, to deal fairly with one another, and to support each other in business ventures. Such teachings could not have been more important since slavery not only forced scores of African Americans into situations of dependency but also robbed them of the capacity to establish a strong economic base for themselves and their descendants. This sense of being powerless compelled black churches, along with mutual aid societies and Masonic orders, to take the lead in establishing 'an economic ethos for the uplift of the race.'[30]

Not only did the Black Church develop an economic ethos, but it also assumed the primary position of leadership for the Black Community on several counts. The Church had to help provide "shelter in the time of storm" for African American families that were facing the barrage of assaults to their being and determination to be free. This can be referred to as the "refuge" function of the "invisible institution." The Church served as the agent and advocate for Black abolition and autonomy. This can be referred to as the "liberation" function of the Church. The Church also functioned as the instrument of social advancement and economic viability. This can be referred to as the "uplift" or "elevation" function of the church. As Wilmore states:

> The primary impulse behind these Northern (church) developments was a desire not so much for survival...but for autonomy, racial solidarity, self-help, and individual and group elevation. Thus Peter Spencer formed a new denomination, the Union Church of African Members, in Wilmington, Delaware, in 1818; Richard Allen became the first bishop of the African Methodist Episcopal Church, founded in Philadelphia in 1816; and James Varick became the first bishop of the African Methodist Episcopal Zion Church, founded in New York City in 1821. These men, together with Absalom Jones, rector of St. Thomas Episcopal Church of Africans in Philadelphia; John Gloucester, pastor of the First African Presbyterian Church of the same city; Peter Williams, Jr., the first ordained black priest of the Episcopal Church in New York; and Thomas Paul, the founder of the first black Baptist Church, also in New York City, were all strong, progressive leaders who, in the first two decades

---

30   Baldwin, 21.

of the nineteenth century, promoted education and social betterment as a religious obligation. [31]

The Black Church was firmly established as the one institution that had a direct connection to the daily experiences of African American communities that were seeking to anchor themselves in the new "Promised Land" of the North. Many parishioners had migrated to the North with a religious sensibility infused with an objective of social mobility. They had seen the Church as the host and sponsor of educational programs, communal gatherings, civic organizations and fraternal associations. Black elementary schools were hosted in churches. Black colleges were founded by and in Black Churches. Respected organizations such as the NAACP and Urban League met in the fellowship halls of churches. This all helped to shape an institutional mindset that was germane to religious life. However, it did not erase the systemic racism that was manifested in de facto segregation, which solidified and reified classism. It became increasingly difficult to discern and advance the tripartite mission of survival, elevation and liberation. Some restructuring needed to occur to facilitate the shifts occurring in Black economic life. As Wilmore states:

> Between the First and Second World Wars it was necessary to realign the survival, elevation, and liberation themes so as to create the kind of balance and harmony between them that would be conducive to racial advancement. It was the experience of African American leadership during the era of abolitionism and missionary emigrationism that when one of these themes or tendencies is either neglected or exaggerated above the other two, the result is that commitment to the biblical God and to a militant church, on the one hand, and to African American political, economic, and cultural life, on the other, fall apart. The center collapses, and chaos reigns. This happened during the Radical Reconstruction and again during the Great Depression of the 1930s. On both occasions the consequence was a kind of racial schizophrenia that left the masses in moral confusion and the middle classes in a spiritual malaise that rendered them powerless to give the kind of leadership necessary for

---

31   Wilmore, *Pragmatic Spirituality*, 52-3.

realignment and a new beginning as soon as relative calm and prosperity returned.[32]

The Modern Civil Rights Movement became the ferment necessary to awaken the African American consciousness for the need to galvanize its base and resources in order to build the new Promised Land. The 1954 Brown versus Board of Education Supreme Court decision became the precursor to the deconstruction of institutional and systemic barriers to racial equality. This helped to give impetus to Montgomery Bus Boycott and the legal removal of racial segregation in public accommodations. This, in turn, gave the Black Church the springboard for a return to its radical and practical roots of racial advancement. Wilmore goes on to say:

> Beginning in 1955 the genius of Martin Luther King, Jr. brought the three motifs or traditions (survival, elevation and liberation) together again in a prophetic combination that wedded the deep spirituality and will to survive of the alienated and impoverished masses with the sophisticated pragmatism and determination to achieve equality and complete liberation that characterized the parvenu urbanites and the "New Negro" intelligentsia of the Harlem Renaissance. King embraced all three of these tendencies and created a multidimensional movement, inseparable from the African American church but not subservient to it. As a young Baptist preacher he set in motion social, political, economic, religious, and cultural forces that have not yet run their full course. Martin Luther King Jr. stands, therefore, at the pinnacle of African American religious and political developments in the twentieth century.[33]

The Civil Rights Movement laid the foundation for a new Black Church. A heightened level of Black consciousness, infused with an Africentric pride was related to a new sense of responsibility to the African American community. The assassination of King in 1968 precipitated Black angst and rage that led to riots and white flight. However, Black Churches had already begun to resume the role of facilitator of social and economic progress. Urban metropolises such as Baltimore saw a resurgence of Black religious leadership. Marion Orr in *Black Social Capital: the Politics of School Reform in Baltimore, 1986-1998* recounts:

---
32 Ibid., 55-6.
33 Ibid., 56.

In the 1950s and 1960s, when the national civil rights movement began in earnest, Baltimore had already established a foundation for an independent African-American protest movement. Black Baltimoreans had 'leaders who had been toughened rather than demoralized by degradation. They had the *Afro-American*, probably the strongest black newspaper in the United States...They had strong churches under politically minded ministers, and they had some aggressive female leaders like Lillie May Jackson and her daughters. Led largely by prominent black middle-class professionals, they accomplished some impressive victories: concessions from private employers for jobs, equalization of pay for black school teachers, significant increases in black voter registration, and the hiring of black police officers.[34]

The aftermath of the riots and the devolution of the Civil Rights movement left Baltimore's Black clergy and other leaders with a quandary in terms of community survival. The invasion-succession of former Jewish communities was plowing toward an inevitable fulfillment. The Palm Sunday weekend of 1968 devastated the city. Antero Pietila also recalls that during the three nights of mayhem, six people died, seven hundred were injured, and over a thousand arrested. Businesses were ransacked, looted, and destroyed. He writes that when "Anguish gripped America's devastated cities. To prevent a race war, Congress enacted the Civil Rights Act of 1968, including provisions for fair housing."[35] He further notes:

> Few thought that such a measure had a chance when President Johnson had proposed it two years earlier. But with big cities in flames, the House passed the act by a vote of 250 to 172, and the Senate by 71 to 20. Eight days after Dr. King's assassination, President Johnson signed it into law. He engineered the passage so swiftly that Coretta King and many other civil rights leaders were missing from the crowd of 350 guests who witnessed the bill's signing at the hastily arranged East Room ceremony. The White House could not locate them at the time, and the signing could not be delayed. "Fair housing for all—all human beings who live in this

---

34 Marion Orr, *Black Social Capital: The Politics of School Reform in Baltimore, 1986-1998* (Lawrence, KS: University of Kansas Press, 1999), 35.
35 Antero Pietila, *Not in My Neighborhood: How Bigotry Shaped a Great American City* (Chicago: Ivan R. Dee Publishers, 2010), 196.

country—is now part of the American way of life," President Johnson proclaimed.[36]

In 1970s, many Black Churches had to reevaluate their strategies of services to African American families and communities, especially as government sponsored urban renewal programs pumped resources into city domains. History was about to be rewritten in the aftermath of the Civil Rights movement. Some churches retreated into self-preservation or fled to the suburbia, while others began to transform their ministries into community-centered hubs. Harold McDougall reveals that the response of African American churches to urban renewal was to embark on community improvement in the areas of rent-control, government-subsidized housing, and community management of government services. He states that "Social activists, including clergy, turned to the creation of parallel institutions at the neighborhood level to try to repair some of the damage that had been done to the vernacular community by overcrowding, state repression, and the loss of middle-class residents.[37]

Black churches that began to mobilize community-centered ministries merged their historical roles of "all-comprehending" institutions with contemporary genres of church-based organizing, like that promoted by legendary leader Saul Alinsky, and church-based community development, like that promoted by Rev. John Perkins. Both of them were influenced by the Civil Rights movement's grass-roots character and religious spirit. Both of them concluded that government programs were inadequate. Alinsky's Industrial Areas Foundation (IAF) helped to organize BUILD (Baltimoreans United in Leadership Development), a coalition of churches established by IAF in the early 1980s committed to community empowerment. Although IAF is not an African American organization *per se*, it found its greatest early successes in Black communities. The Black Church had the primary role in organizing these neighborhoods. McDougall states:

> The IAF has adopted the position that the church is the primary mediating institution in the black community. Unions, schools, and ethnic clubs, all of which surfaced in the black communities like Old

---

36 *Not in My Neighborhood: How Bigotry Shaped a Great American City*, 196.
37 McDougall, 98-106.

West Baltimore, are now on the decline. The church is the last link with the vernacular community, but even in the black church there are strong counter-pressures. A process of divestment is going on, Reverend Dobson (former pastor of Union Baptist Church) observed. "First the white congregations divested and moved to the suburbs, leaving behind some very fine buildings that black congregations took over. But now the black congregations want to move to the suburbs, too. The ministers are trying to invest in the community, to make it difficult for the congregation to leave. They believe that spiritual growth takes place in the 'community of need,' with all its pain and danger, rather in a withdrawn, pristine, monastic sort of spiritual experience way out in the suburbs."[38]

BUILD found a great deal of success primarily because of its emphasis upon galvanizing and mobilizing "community." This squares directly with the core identity of the African American community and the Black Church. IAF helped the Black Church, in a sense, return to its African-centered roots. Cadres of church members were equipped to do social and political analyses of the state of inner-city communities. They were then empowered to do "actions" on politicians, landlords and business owners that were violating an ethic of community accountability. BUILD gained headway in a few city neighborhoods. However, many of the neighborhoods that saw a resurgence in the 1980s in the BUILD movement and in the administration of the first Black mayor, Kurt Schmoke, have once again experienced great disinvestment and decay.

A disciple of the civil rights movement in the South was Reverend John Perkins. Perkins embraced and espoused the concept of King's "Beloved Community," promoting it as a possible reality in poor communities across America. A young leader in Mississippi the 1960s, Perkins was dramatically influenced by the work of the Student Non-violent Coordinating Committee (SNCC) and the Congress on Racial Equality (CORE). However, he believed that these organizations were not as committed to King's vision of true racial cooperation and grass roots empowerment. He saw a new vision of community. Charles Marsh writes:

---

[38] McDougall, 133-34.

Perkins charted a new course for building beloved community in America—one that defied conventional political categories. Leadership must be based in poor communities and eventually rise out of these communities, but at the same time outsiders would be invited to play a critical role in fostering indigenous leadership. In Perkins' view, civil rights organizations such as SNCC and CORE too often racialized and politicized the role of the outsider at the expense of the well-being of people in poor communities. Patronization is a worry only when outsiders fail to discern the gifts of the poor, their loyalty, fragility, creativity, and holiness, and to accept the authority of black leadership—that is, when outsiders fail to appreciate the diverse gifts of the body of Christ and the mutuality ingredient in redemptive community. Without backing away from his support of integration, equal opportunity, affirmative action, and welfare—but recognizing their incompleteness—Perkins further concluded that government programs alone failed to address the deeper sources of hopelessness in black communities... The civil rights movement had focused its energies on legal injustice—as the times required—but it failed to offer a compelling account of the spiritual energies and disciplines required to sustain beloved community and thus failed to give detail and depth to a "holistic Gospel." The civil rights movement failed to reckon with the truth that personal salvation is the most enduring source of social engagement, care for the poor, costly forgiveness, and reparations for slavery.[39]

Perkins went on to lead a movement that was grassroots, indigenous and neighborhood based. Starting with local community development organizations, he began to coalesce with leaders in other cities that had adopted his conceptual framework for community transformation. Marsh describes the impact of Perkins and the organization:

> In 1989 [Perkins] formed the Christian Community Development Association (CCDA), the organizational infrastructure of the faith-based community-building movement. In its first year, the CCDA comprised 200 individuals and 37 organizational members. At a recent CCDA

---

[39] Charles Marsh, *The Beloved Community: How Faith Shapes Social Justice, From the Civil Rights Movement to Today* (New York: Basic Books, 2005), 176-77.

conference, Perkins announced organizations with sites in more than 100 cities, including Bethel New Life, a comprehensive community development initiative in Chicago, and Habitat for Humanity…Annual meetings of the Christian Community Development Association resemble a mix of mass meeting, Billy Graham crusade, and SNCC planning session circa 1963. Between worship services, prayer meetings and Gospel songs are seminars on community organizing; tutorials on writing applications for public sector grants; support groups for partnering with corporations and affluent churches; and nuts-and-bolts instruction on starting public health centers, running after-school tutorial programs, transforming crack houses into "Kingdom houses," and managing volunteers and prison aftercare. Perkins has extended SCLC's model of community mobilizing and SNCC's preference for community organizing to a distinctive theological vision of community building—activism mindful of the three Rs of relocation, reconciliation, and redistribution, the ingredients of holistic faith.[40]

Perkins gospel had reached the city of Baltimore by 1986 when Mark Gornik, a young Presbyterian minister and his best friend Allan Tibbles moved into a row house in the Baltimore neighborhood of Sandtown-Winchester.[41] "As white Christians, we believed it was vital that we turn from our complicity in a culture that is anti-black, anti-poor and anti-urban and turn to the biblical obligations of justice and reconciliation. We came to listen, to learn, to build friendships, and to live out our faith. When people would ask us, 'What are you doing here?' our answer was always the same: 'We are here to be neighbors.'"[42] After training with Perkins' organization, Gornik and Tibbles took steps to establish a church-based community development enterprise that included housing, church and school. Marsh describes their evolution:

> In time, Gornik's row house on Mount Street and Tibbel's on Stricker became the two bases of a twelve-block "focus area" called New Song Community. With strong neighborhood leadership and financial support from Baltimore churches and philanthropic organizations, a slate of holistic programs was created under the auspices of New

---
40 Ibid., 184-5.
41 Ibid., 190.
42 Ibid., 190.

Song Community Ministries: a health center, job-placement program, private Christian school, legal cooperative, youth services cooperative, community church, and a Habitat for Humanity project, which Jimmy Carter launched himself on a festive spring day in 1992. Establishing the church was a decisive step in anchoring the ministry in the community, since many of the community-building initiatives that survive the first blush of excitement are based in common worship. All these commitments have formed the context within which Gornik thinks theologically.[43]

New Song Community and the Christian Community Development Corporation have the ingredients of an Africentric praxis model for community empowerment. They have recaptured a radical zeal akin to the Black churches of the mid-twentieth century that provided a range of social services for African Americans while working arduously against the sting of white racism and economic injustice. Most of the principles of the Nguzu Saba are apparent in the goals and objectives of CCDA. Such an intersection between the truly grassroots Christian aims and Africentric principles of community make for a powerful foundation for community transformation.

---

[43] Ibid., 195.

CHAPTER FOUR
THERE IS A BALM:
THE BLACK CHURCH'S DUAL ROLE OF RECONCILIATION AND RESTORATION

There is a balm in Gilead to heal a sin-sick soul.
There is a balm in Gilead to make the wounded whole.
Traditional African American spiritual

Given the often tenuous encounter of Africans in America throughout history, the themes of survival and liberation have best described the dual role of the Black Church for centuries. A major concern of scholars in the field of Black Congregational Studies is the emerging chasm between the Black Church and the African American community, socially, spiritually, psychologically and physically. The causes of this rupture are debatable. What is nearly unanimous is the fact that this reality is leaving the community without one of its most important resources for survival and progress. The interplay of survival and liberation is summarized explicitly in the work of Carroll A. Watkins Ali, a Black Womanist pastoral theologian who provides the following working definitions:

> ....*survival* is the ability of African Americans (1) to resist systematic oppression and genocide and (2) to recover the self, which entails a psychological recovery from the abuse and dehumanization of political oppression and exploitation as well as recovery of African heritage, culture, and values that were repressed during slavery. By *liberation*, I mean (1) total freedom from all kinds of oppression for African descendants of slaves and (2) the ability of African Americans as a people to self-determine and engage in the process of transformation of the dominant oppressive culture through political resistance.[44]

---

44 Carroll A. Watkins Ali, *Survival & Liberation: Pastoral Theology in African American Context*, St. Louis: Chalice Press, 1999, 2.

Survival and liberation of African Americans are urgent pastoral theological concerns.[45] Watkins Ali's work sheds light on the role of the church as an agent of pastoral caregiving to persons who are experiencing the ravaging effects of socio-economic racism and injustice, especially in the abject poverty of inner city ghettos. Watkins Ali describes the contemporary African American context:

> The current situation facing African Americans is indicative of the fact that the racist backlash has again effectively undermined the progress of the Black struggle. Collectively, the state of Black Americans...is still quite critical. On the whole, African Americans have not been able to overcome the effects of systematic racism. Today the majority of African Americans live under conditions of genocidal poverty. Systematic racism has prevented Blacks from being able to amass an economic base that would ensure that Blacks, as a people, are not disproportionately filling the prisons, unemployed, underemployed, and undereducated, forced to comply with welfare systems, and living in ghettos as we currently are.[46]

While Watkins Ali highlights the deleterious effects of systemic racism on economic, social upward mobility, other scholars point to the need to repair two major breaches in the African American world: between the Black Church and the African American community, and between the Black Church and Black theology. The two themes that describe the prescriptive actions of this study have been incorporated as *reconciliation* and *restoration*. The African American community, ironically in post-integration America, appears to be more fractured than the period of racial segregation. The socio-economic class divisions have become more pronounced, and the Black Church has not been exempt. Many Black Churches have become indifferent, if not hostile, to the persons who dwell in the very neighborhoods in which their edifices are located. The Church should be a necessary ally and agent of liberation for poor, struggling and fractured families. However, the Afrocentric perspectives of culturally-relevant and socially-conscious Black churches are models for redemption. This should be the aim of the prophetic Black Church that is called for in most of the works reviewed. Watkins Ali goes on to say:

---

45 Ibid., 3,
46 Ibid., 26-27.

In light of the potential of African cultural heritage for healing, sustaining, guiding, nurturing, empowering, and liberating African Americans spiritually and psychologically, it is also incumbent upon pastoral theology to reflect upon *reconciling* ministry in a new light. In this respect, reconciling in the African American context is an act of reclaiming, restoring and retaining African philosophy and culture in ministry to African Africans. Reconciling in this respect is also an act of reconciling African Americans to African Americans. That is, reconciling middle-class African Americans to under-class African Americans, and reconciling that eliminates fratricide among African Americans, which has reached epidemic proportions. This is a vital element in the survival and liberation of African Americans.[47]

The chasm between Black Theology and the Black Church has been chronicled *ad nauseam*. Black theologians have charged that black churches have abandoned their liberation history in favor of an "ineffectual spirituality" and have abnegated their role and responsibility to confront the racial and economic oppression being experienced by Black people.[48] Black churches responded by critiquing the Black Theology project as being reductionist and divisive, favoring Black power to the neglect of the message of the Christian message of universal love.[49] Black pastoral theologian and homiletician Dale P. Andrews has called the charge by Black theologians a matter of a "missed diagnosis" that has either overlooked or underestimated the power of American individualism on the psyche and practices of African Americans. A Christian social ethics bridge must be built that helps to move people between personal faith and social justice. A return to an Africentric concept of communal responsibility, including social service and social justice, is possible when the dialogue between Black Theology and the Black Church is mutual, organic, and practical.

Most authors of studies focusing on the Black Church will concur that the shifting away from the prophetic, liberation ethic of the Black Church. This is a response of two main factors, the impact of American individualism and, consequently, the "bifurcation of the Black community."[50] As Andrews says:

---
47 Ibid., 121-22.
48 Dale P. Andrews, *Practical Theology for Black Churches*, Louisville: Westminster John Knox Press, 2002, 4.
49 Ibid., 4.
50 Ibid., 62.

As black churches focus preaching and pastoral ministries on personal salvation, inner spirituality, and religious piety, the ideology of American individualism invades their sense of corporate identity and communal responsibility. The disruption of corporate identity and communal responsibility only increases amid the struggles for socioeconomic advancement conditioned by individualism in a systemically racist society.[51]

I advocate for a practical or pragmatic approach to ministry in the context of the African American community that is both spiritually and socially liberating. This resonates in an Africentric spirituality that draws from the rich cultural heritage of the motherland and appropriates it in the contemporary *sitz im leben*. James Evans seeks to make Black pastoral theology more focused on America's most pressing problems, such as racism, poverty, shame, disease and dysfunctional families, probing to their deepest cultural and religious roots in order to bring healing and liberation through ministries of grace, salvation and solidarity. Conversely, J. Deotis Roberts, one of the "fathers" of Black theology, is pressed to articulate the theological demands of the church leadership as ministers of reconciliation who educate and empower congregants to be a "prophethood" of all believers, requiring repentance, forgiveness and cross-bearing.

There are several actual examples of culturally-relevant, socially-conscious congregations that have been spotlighted in the various studies that were reviewed. In fact, Julia Speller observes a few congregations primarily from an Africentric perspective. Speller notes:

> …a representative sample of these faith communities who have adopted a both/and rather than an either/or posture in balancing their culture and faith. In their ministries, they simultaneously hear, acknowledge, and walk to the rhythm of the drums within but also talk through their congregational life and mission in the words of a liberating gospel that brings life, healing and empowerment. This book will, consequently, profile congregations that have found ways to ignite congregational vitality and sharpen Christian witness through an Africentric spirituality.[52]

---
51 Ibid., 58.
52 Julia Speller, *Walkin' the Talk: Keepin' the Faith in Africentric Congregations*, Cleveland: Pilgrim Press, 2005, xiii.

To be sure, not all self-identified Africentric congregations are doing community development work and not all congregations that are doing community development are Africentric. However, there is a distinctive correlation between Africentric spirituality and ministries of empowerment and liberation. There appears to be a burden in Africentric churches to make a difference in the conditions of the people in their environs, with a global perspective of pain, suffering and injustice that should be alleviated through ministries of transformation. Nile Harper in *Urban Churches, Vital Signs: beyond Charity towards Justice* in a congregational study discerns a similar set of themes. Of the twenty-eight congregations that Harper studied, an overwhelming majority of them were predominantly African American. Those that were not African American shared some common beliefs about the sanctity of community, the spirit of shared resources and responsibilities, and the sacredness of a shared story. Harper evinces that "an affirmation that innovative, constructive, and faithful ministry is taking place in urban churches, and that his ministry is of such great importance to the life of American Christianity that it should be widely shared.[53] Harper's work is consistent with much of the research about socially-responsible and culturally relevant congregations. Their work is:

- Creating more culturally appropriate worship
- Creating more inclusive, spiritually mature community
- Nurturing faith that engages the challenges of city life
- Reaching out to make global connections for peace and justice
- Finding effective ways to nurture and mentor children and youth
- Inventing constructive ways of redeveloping neighborhoods
- Promoting the redevelopment of affordable housing
- Enabling people to recover from destructive addictions
- Strengthening family life spiritually, socially, and economically
- Forming partnerships for resource development
- Developing community-based schools[54]

Finally, the pioneering work of Rev. John Perkins and his Christian Community Development Association (CCDA) gives an organizational framework for the genre. Most Black Churches have done successful

---

53 Nile Harper, *Urban Churches, Vital Signs: Beyond Charity towards Justice*, Eugene, Oregon: Wipf and Stock Publishers, 1999, xiv.
54 Ibid., xiv.

community development work without the guidance of the CCDA. However, the CCDA association has helped to mobilize numerous faith-based CDC's and galvanize large resources, financial and material, to help transform many urban neighborhoods. Furthermore, two of Perkins' works, *Restoring At-Risk Communities* and *With Justice for All*, share the gospel of Christian community development and espouse the principles and philosophy of the movement. The principles are: Relocation, Living among the People, Reconciliation, Redistribution (Just Distribution of Resources), Leadership Development, Listening to Community, Church-Based, Wholistic Approach, and Empowerment. These principles are related and translatable to the Nguzo Saba principles of Africentric cultural life and spirituality.

CHAPTER FIVE
BLOW THE TRUMPET IN ZION: THE ROLE OF BLACK THEOLOGY

Blow the trumpet in Zion, consecrate a fast, call a sacred assembly.
Gather the people, sanctify the congregation, assemble the elders,
gather the children and nursing babies; let the bridegroom
go out from his chamber, and the bride from her dressing room.
Joel 2:15-16

Restoring the historic, integral connection of the Black Church and the African American community is both a theological and missional goal. The proponents of Black theology would argue that they are one and the same. At its heart, Black theology is practical, and its ultimate aim is liberation of the oppressed. The subjects and objects of liberation are people who live in communities that have been marginalized by racial, political and economic injustice. This has been the historical role of the Black Church, which is located almost exclusively in predominantly African American communities. However, that role has been diminished by the continuing confluence of religious and social assimilation in post-Civil Rights American society, and institutional self-preservation and apathy in the Black Church. Many Black Churches have fallen short in their commitment to liberation and social change.

Black theology was forged in the crucible of the Civil Rights Movement of the 50's and 60's and really emerged in the aftermath of the assassination of Dr. Martin Luther King, Jr. in 1968. It rode the wave of the Black Church's principal role in the movement while also finding voice in the Black Power movement's critique of reticent and non-concerned Black Churches. This highlighted a growing disconnect – theologically and practically – between the academy of Black theologians and grassroots Black Churches, between the interpretation of Black faith and the actual practice of ministry. Black theologians were espousing a political agenda that took the power structures to task, including, and especially, the Church. Dale Andrews discusses the disconnect of Black Churches with their communities:

> In a short period of time, the rhetoric of this political agenda echoed at the center of an emerging chasm between the black theology project and black churches. A principal disparity emerged between their respective theological interpretations of faith and ministry. On the one hand, the black theology project regarded black churches as spiritually removed or "otherworldly." In July of 1966, for example, the newly organized National Committee of Negro Churchmen issued a statement on black power: 'Too often the Negro Church has stirred (sic) its members away from the reign of God in *this world* to a distorted and complacent view of *an otherworldly* conception of God's power.' With such claims, proponents of black theology addressed the message of the Black Power Movement to black churches. Black theologians charged that black churches had abandoned their liberation history for an ineffectual spirituality, and therefore failed to confront adequately the concerns of black people living under racial and economic oppression.[55]

The truth is that Black theology would not exist without the Black Church. As a product of the mission of the Black Church, a unique pastoral theology emerged to enable the dual roles of survival and liberation for African American people. Carroll Watkins-Ali describes both as necessary functions of pastoral theology in the Black Church:

> *Survival* is the ability of African Americans (1) to resist systematic oppression and genocide and (2) to recover the self, which entails a psychological recovery from the abuse and dehumanization of political oppression and exploitation as well as recovery of African heritage, culture and values that were repressed during slavery. By *liberation*, I mean (1) total freedom from all kinds of oppression for African descendants of slaves and (2) the ability of African Americans as a people to self-determine and engage in the process of transformation of the dominant oppressive culture through political resistance.[56]

---

55 Dale Andrews, *Practical Theology for Black Churches* (Louisville: Westminster John Knox, 2002), 3-4.
56 Carroll A. Watkins-Ali, *Survival and Liberation: Pastoral Theology in African American Context* (St. Louis: Chalice Press, 1999), 2.

Watkins-Ali argues for a Black pastoral theology that is defined as "theological reflection on the experience of the cultural context as relevant for strategic pastoral caregiving in the context of ministry...It suggests that pastoral theological reflection is at least a two-step process that puts the experience of the people inhabiting the context for ministry ahead of the experience of the pastoral caregiver in the ministry context."[57]

The current context of ministry for African Americans has been described by Watkins-Ali as "genocidal poverty." It is "the kind of living conditions that are responsible for the growing death rate in the Black community. Although poverty is not normally listed as a cause of death, the malnutrition, fetal demise, untreated disease (due to lack of or poor health care), homicide, fratricide, suicide and alcohol and drug abuse that are becoming prevalent in poor Black communities all contribute to the gradual form of genocide that has been integral to the systematic racial oppression of Blacks."[58] The Black Church, especially in urban areas, must begin to work towards alleviating and eradicating this persistent condition. However, it will require a recovery of an African-centered theology that is practical and intentional. This cannot happen without progressive and responsible leadership, especially from theologian/practitioners. James A. Harris highlights the ambiguity of the Black pastor as theologian:

> It is the understanding of God and the world that governs the life and work of the pastor and parishioners. Being a pastor is a calling! It requires an inordinate amount of love and sacrifice because the work of the pastor is often thankless and extremely demanding. It is also a constant struggle that involves motivation, change, continuity, teaching, preaching, counseling, managing, and a host of other skills, emotions, and activities. The pastor is admired and hated, trusted and distrusted, supported and repudiated. The pastor is both prophet and politician—balancing life and work between theory and practice. He or she must have a vision of ministry and a plan for accomplishing that vision through the people who constitute the church and community…If every black preacher in America decided to confront seriously the status quo through sermons and programs that advocated protest against our cavalier treatment of the poor, we could begin the process of transforming the condition of

---
57   Ibid., 10-11.
58   Ibid., 25.

life for the oppressed of society. This radical approach to ministry would enable the church to reclaim its heritage as an institution that has been on the cutting edge of social change.[59]

Harris goes on to talk about the mutual interdependence of the Church and the community, pointing out that "the economic survivability of the church and the community is grounded in a mutual understanding of the need to help each other advance beyond their present status."[60] As has been stated, one cannot understand the Black Church without placing it within the context of the African American community, with its values of self-worth, mutual care, and shared responsibility. Dale Andrews draws on the work of Pastoral theologian Ed Wimberly and his concept of "narrative hermeneutics."[61] According to Andrews, "Because of the narrative character, African American pastoral care for the individual thrives in community. The hermeneutical process for personal wholeness is a communal process of mutual storytelling. This reflexive process includes interpretation and reinterpretation between individual experiences and those experiences common to the culture or faith community itself."[62] He further notes, "Because of the respect for personal experience, the communal hermeneutic does allow for new encounters and new interpretations of meaning. The community of faith is therefore expanded by the introduction of new experiences. What I find particularly vital here is the evolving character of corporate care. Corporate care is mutual care only so long as it is not stagnant. Instead, it thrives in a dynamic interplay between traditional narratives, narratives of the local community, and individual narratives or experiences.[63] In the "communal hermeneutic," Wimberly is describing an organic, fundamental practice of religious formation that happens in faith communities. This practice is not usually formal or academic.

Gayraud Wilmore observes a "second level of understanding" of Black theology that has "no interest in developing a polemical response to the Euro-American synthesis of Christian truth in the context of Euro-American experience but has another purpose instead. At this level we are not concerned about the ontological and soteriological meaning of blackness but rather about

---

59 James A. Harris, *Pastoral Theology: A Black Church Perspective* (Minneapolis: Fortress Press 1991), ix, 16.
60 Ibid., 37.
61 Andrews, 25.
62 Ibid.
63 Ibid., 25.

recovering the simple truth about God, Jesus Christ, and the Holy Spirit which African American Christians have taken for granted in relation to themselves from slavery to the present day."[64] This is more a "folk theology" or a religion of the people. This is a crucial concept because it provides a space for the establishment of a "common ground" for conversation and collaboration between the church and the community.

The Black Church has functioned somewhat like what Walter Brueggemann describes as an "alternative community."[65] This alternative community has been characterized by prophetic ministry. "The task of prophetic ministry," according to Brueggeman, "is to nurture, nourish, and evoke a consciousness and perception alternative to the consciousness and perception of the dominant culture around us."[66] An Africentric spirituality recovers a cultural ethos that counters the effects of racism, classism and oppression. Brueggemann argues:

> The alternative consciousness to be nurtured, on the one hand, serves to *criticize* in dismantling the dominant consciousness. To that extent, it attempts to do what the liberal tendency has done: engage in a rejection and delegitimizing of the present ordering of things. On the other hand, that alternative consciousness to be nurtured serves to *engergize* persons and communities by its promise of another time and situation toward which the community of faith may move. To that extent, it attempts to do what the conservative tendency has done, to live in fervent anticipation of the newness that God has promised and will surely give.[67]

Although Black theology is a primary source of information and inspiration for prophetic ministry, it is not without valid criticism, especially from a truly Afrocentric perspective. Much of Black theology, at least its categories of description, has been drawn from Eurocentric concepts of theological inquiry which in themselves have been deleterious to Black fulfillment and self-determination. Andrews perceives that the challenge now involves, "re-addressing black theology to Black churches" and notes that it will require a redirection of "black theology's experiences of Christianity as well as the human encounter with oppression in black life." Such an approach would

---
64   Wilmore, *Pragmatic Spirituality*, 159.
65   Walter Brueggemann, *The Prophetic Imagination* (Minneapolis: Fortress Press, 2001), 3.
66   Ibid., 3.
67   Ibid., 3.

require "Black theology to interpret theological concepts that presently exist in black churches." However, he cautions that "in the process of interpretation, black theologians must not dismiss the churches' own conceptualizations or theological criteria."[68]

Many theologians have countered Black theology's assumptions of inherent relevance to the African American community by pointing out the lack of an Africentric focus. Cecil Cone contends that the starting point for Black theology should be Black folk religion, which has its roots in African culture. Failure to start from this religious trajectory leads to an identity confusion for Black theology.[69] Andrews picks up on this point: "This critique insists that black theologians re-conceptualize their treatment of liberation from within black folk religion. Such an effort might provide a more critical tool for the very faithfulness to social action among black churches that black theology aspires to advance."[70]

The Black Church has been impacted, as has the African American community en masse, by American individualism. Many Black theologians have vehemently articulated this truth. A few have addressed this dilemma through a theological conceptualization of a return "home." This home is at once spiritual, cultural and physical. The perceived separation between the Black Church and the African American community has left both entities as "aliens" in a strange land. Butler verifies the breach but insists that ending the separation requires reclamation of the African American spiritual legacy which he believes will provide us with a "complete sense of self" and lead to liberation. [71]

Homer Ashby, Jr. continues the theme by "conjuring" a new Promised Land for the African American community that is led by the "Joshua Church," which actualizes African-American identified ministries of survival and liberation. This includes a recovery of self, freedom from all kinds of oppression and the ability to self-determine.[72] The Promised Land for African Americans is just as it was for Joshua and the children of Israel – a return home. Ashby writes:

> The Promised Land for blacks today needs to be found in an internal consciousness. This internal consciousness is characterized by an increased sensitivity to the threat of extinction, the restoration of a sense

---

68 Andrews, 50.
69 Cecil Cone, *Identity Crisis*, 18.
70 Andrews, 51.
71 Butler, 68.
72 Homer U. Ashby, Jr., *Our Home is Over Jordan: A Black Pastoral Theology* (St. Louis: Chalice Press, 2003), 37.

of collective identity, engagement in an ongoing struggle beyond mere survival, and partnership with God in whom the will and the guarantee of the promise are located.[73]

The Promised Land for blacks in the twenty-first century is a place that exists within the larger American society and its culture but at the same time maintains a separate existence. This separate existence is more attitudinal than spatial. The Promised Land is an attitude, a way of being, a responsive resistance, but yet an a priori declaration of what it means to be black in America. Such a promised land is rooted in the promise, will, and guarantee of God. The promise is that African Americans as a people can live a life with full humanity, that God will supply that power and the will for black people to struggle in this conquest, and that the victory of full humanity is guaranteed even in the face of a hostile, death-dealing environment.[74]

The recovery of an Africentric identity and ethic for ministry is a journey home. This journey will require a fight for freedom - liberation. The liberation motif is an indispensable aspect of the Black Church's struggle to rebuild community. Because of the pervasive nature of racial injustice, liberation is a necessary partner to the survival aspect of ministry in African American communities. Dennis Proctor, A.M.E. Zion Bishop and former pastor of Pennsylvania Avenue Church, lists four important points of the liberation motif:

1. A liberation motif that is affirming would benefit the religious and non-religious persons in the Afro-American community helping to create a climate of cooperation and inter-dependence to combat the nihilistic threat.
2. Polity and theology aside, African Americans share biogenetic commonality and history of oppression and repression that necessitate common survival mechanisms and doctrinal development.
3. The community of faith, be it Christian, Muslim, African, Traditional or other, share the same heroes and heroines of the struggle.
4. The rise of independent African churches in America was not the result of theological or ecclesiastical differences but racial prejudice and discrimination.[75]

---
73 Ibid., 27.
74 Ibid., 31.
75 Dennis Proctor, *A Strategy for Recovering the Liberation Motif of the African Methodist Episcopal Zion Church* (Unpublished D.Min. Thesis, United Theological Seminary, Dayton, Ohio 1993), 10-11.

The twenty-first century Black Church should recognize that our current social location is not a matter of theology but sociology, precipitated by racial and social injustice. The resurgence of the prophetic Black Church of the past will be initiated and activated by a recovery of the African spirituality that shaped the original Black Church in America. Peter Paris identifies six moral virtues of African and African American churches that promote community and appear to be preeminent in both. They are: 1. Beneficence: The beneficent person is a person of good will, one who joyfully extends hospitality to all alike, respecting all persons. 2. Forbearance: This is a patient tolerance to do what is necessary to preserve life under caustic conditions. 3. Practical Wisdom: "This is an excellence of that thought that guides good action." "It is the fully developed capacity of a free moral agent for making reasonable judgments about the best means for the attainment of penultimate goals as well as the determination of their commensurability with the ultimate goal of the good life." 4. Improvisation: This brings novelty to bear on the familiar, not for the sake of destroying the latter, but for the purpose of heightening the individuality and uniqueness of the agent and his or her creative ability. 5. Forgiveness: This rebukes the toll that hatred can exact by cultivating the habitual exercise of kindness for the sake of the community. 6. Justice: This is realized in two ways – the individual's obligations to the community as mediated through the many dealing individuals have with one another and the community's obligations to its members and itself.[76]

An African centered spirituality is best suited to the Black Church's goals of reconciling and restoring the African American community. The moral virtues of the culture and adapted principles of Nguzo Saba are the effectual ingredients of a redeemed and revitalized neighborhood. Considering the fact that Dr. Martin Luther King, Jr. was the product of the Black Church and the African American community, it is no wonder that his vision of a Beloved Community incorporated, implicitly and explicitly, much of these same characteristics. This indeed provides the foundation for the building of a "holy common ground."

---

76   Paris, 136-153.

CHAPTER SIX
MARCHING TO ZION: THE RELEVANCE OF AN AFRICENTRIC APPROACH TO PROPHETIC ENGAGEMENT

We're marching to Zion, beautiful, beautiful Zion
We're marching upward to Zion
That beautiful city of God.
Traditional Hymn

Afrocentricity[77] is a necessary approach for African Americans dealing with the contemporary predicament of misery and malaise in most urban neighborhoods, overpopulated disproportionately by Black churches on most every corner. There is an explicit perspective necessary for arousing the consciousness of the preacher and the parishioner, the church and the community. Roberts points out that Africentrism provides an alternate conceptual framework that offers the opportunity for African Americans to view reality. The questions that Roberts pose are significant because their focus is empowerment. He notes:

> It entails a serious attempt to understand the manner in which Africans have viewed reality in their context of culture for thousands of years before they encountered the Western worldview. African Americans attempt to recover their classical roots through empathy, knowledge, and experience. Through new looking glasses, we peer into this Africentered world to observe what may be useful in our commitment to Christianity. What is useful? What must be rejected? What will enrich and empower our Christian way of life?[78]

---

77 This term is used interchangeably with Africentricity. Molefi Kete Asante is credited with coining the term *Afro*centricity, purveying the conceptualization. Subsequent scholars have preferred to use *Afri*centricity, seeing as more consistent with the continent of Africa and shunning the temptation to belittle the term associated with a hairstyle – Afro.
78 Ibid.,14.

Roberts' focus on Africentricism is useful in that it connects with the ideological and cultural movement led by Molefi Asante, Professor of African American Studies at Temple University. Africentrism is both a personal self-consciousness and a collective/communal consciousness. Roberts summarizes Asante's Afrocentric project in the following way:

1. We need to begin our cultural view of Africa with a study of Egypt, Nubia, Cush, and other ancient African cultures.
2. We need to be Africa-oriented in our study of data; Africa becomes subject rather than object. We recenter and relocate Africa as subject.
3. We need to lay claim to our own culture. We cannot divest ourselves of culture. We will either participate in our own culture or the culture of someone else.
4. Africentrists accept the multiplicity of cultural centers. They do not negate Eurocentrism except when Eurocentrisim promotes itself as universal.
5. One is to accept the Africentric outlook as a means for both belief and practice.[79]

While Black Theology is a vitally important resource for Black Churches that are true to their mission of liberation, as an academic discipline and practical guide, it is not inclusive of the necessary cultural and historical elements that account for African American identity. Ivan Douglas Hicks, a pastor who obtained his Ph.D. as a student of Molefi Asante, argues that African Americans must recover the Afrocentric cosmology that was resonant in the African ancestors *prior to* the European Slave Trade and forced African migration in America. Hicks contends:

> …One could say that the key problem is summed up as dealing with the apparent contradictions inherent in the social activism of African Americans for liberation from white racial domination and at the same time participating in the practice of what is often claimed to be a white religion. What African American theologians have done in the past is to isolate this predicament and claim to have a Black Theology. The issue with the Black Theology as developed so far is that it does not take into consideration the ideas of agency and African-centeredness that are

---
[79] Ibid.,14.

derived from Afrocentric theory…One should be able to see how the concept of God has been used in the earliest texts as well as the way the divine has been operationalized in human activity.[80]

The Black Church is the cultural and spiritual product of African spirituality. It became the transporter of the creative "soul force" which combated the insidious racism and dehumanization that Africans unwillingly encountered in the Western world. It is miraculous that African Americans were able to survive such gross inhumanity. Before the Black Church became an institution it was a spiritual and theological worldview encapsulated in the hearts and minds of African peoples. Hicks further clarifies:

> We were able to make it on the spiritual reserve of the great and profound religions of Africa. Even though the African enslaved in America was stripped of everything from pride and self-esteem to cultural identity, somehow even the greatest of humiliation and degradation could not force the African to forget the ways and the worship of home. This pulse beat of African spirituality has for the African American Church been an aspect of the church's freedom and expression. African American worship is emotive, poetic and even graceful.[81]

Hicks' focus on Africentricism has led him to present a paradigm for praxis called "Theo-Africology."[82] There are four critical assumptions raised by Hicks in response to the Black Theology Project that has its origins in the 1960s Black Power Movement. First of all, the African American Church has had several surviving Africanisms that correspond to concepts, ideas and styles of the African world.[83] Secondly, the Kemetic (Ancient Egypt) foundation of classical African concepts should be reexamined in their fundamental relationship to ancient Eastern and European concepts. Thirdly, Afrocentric inquiry must be critical of the historical events in the development of the Christian Church and Christian theology. Finally, Hicks proposes a next step for Afrocentric thinking and action:

---

80 Ivan Douglas Hicks, *Centering African American Religion: Toward an Afrocentric Analysis*, A Doctoral Dissertation submitted to Temple University (Ann Arbor, MI: UMI Dissertation Services, 2003), 12.
81 Ibid., 14.
82 *Theo-Africology* is the term coined by Ivan Douglas Hicks. It is the combination of Africalogy and Theology. It seeks to view theology or the study of God through the eyes of the African without regard to transgenerational or transcontinental issues. Ibid., 40.
83 Ibid., 35.

> One of the major dimensions of the development of Theo-Africology would have to be the principle of empowerment…Africological scholarship should not be done simply for the sake of scholarship. There should be a deliberately humane purpose for Theo-Africology.[84]

An Africentric Christianity is embedded in the DNA of the Black Church in America. It is interesting that the first two Black denominations deliberately included the word African in their names: African Methodist Episcopal Church and the African Methodist Episcopal Zion Church (several of the first Black congregations established in America also self-identified as *African*) were both founded in the late eighteenth century in the crucible of American slavery in the South and *de facto* segregation in the North. The founders of these movements merged their own sense of spiritual ethnocentricism alongside their emerging institutional evangelicalism. The two denominations, born out of the hypocrisy of White Christianity exemplified by injustice and inequality of the Methodist Episcopal Church – one of the first religious proponents of the abolition of slavery – brilliantly synthesized a firm understanding of the Gospel of freedom for every person created in the *imago dei* with their own indigenous perception of what C. Eric Lincoln and Lawrence Mamiya called "the Black Sacred Cosmos."[85] The African adherents to the Gospel in America saw an adept way to be true to their "calling" while calling the white Church into account for its complicity with an evil and corrupt system. In *The Black Church in America*, John H. Satterwhite, a former historian of the A.M.E. Zion Church, says:

> African" and "Christian" in the names of our denominations denote that we are always concerned for the well-being of economically and politically exploited persons, for gaining or regaining a sense of our own worth, and for determining our own future. We must never invest with institutions that perpetuate racism. Our churches work for the change of all processes which prevent our members who are victims of racism from participating fully in civic and governmental structures.[86]

---
84 Ibid., 36.
85 C. Eric Lincoln and Lawrence Mamiya , *The Black Church in the African American Experience*, (Durham: Duke University Press, 1990), 2.
86 Ibid., 47.

As the first Black denominations began to assimilate into the mainstream of religious institutionalism in America they emphasized the identifiers of Baptist and Methodist. However, their initial emphasis seemed to be upon their racial/cultural identity as primary self-recognition. Bishop William Jacob Walls, in his expansive history of the A.M.E. Zion Church, deliberately commends the foundation of the denomination in its African origins in civilization and religion as evidenced in the writings and teachings of the prominent "fathers" of the movement. It seems that the early adherents saw their mission as Africans in America to redeem the Church and liberate the world from "defiled" understandings and practices of true Christianity, which had African roots. Bishop Walls cites an African-centered perspective in the work of his early predecessor and champion of the denomination, Bishop James W. Hood, in Hood's book about the history of the Zion Church:

> Ever since Simon the Ethiopian bore the cross of Christ, the Negro, whenever sufficiently enlightened, has stood by it. In Egypt, where Christians have been oppressed for ages, and Christianity has been almost crushed out, the Copts, the descendants of the ancient Egyptians or Mizraimites, still cling to the cross, even in that dark land. While skepticism, Adventism, universalism, annihilationism, probationism, and many other pernicious isms are gaining ground among the white people, the masses of black Christians are still earnestly contending for the faith once delivered to the saints. *It was probably the purpose of Jehovah in maintaining the identity of the race in this country, and forming the African Church, to make it a stronghold of pure and undefiled religion.*[87] (Emphasis added)

This Africentrism emphasized by Bishop Hood highlights the spirituality of African Americans.

Gayraud Wilmore also presents a compelling case for the Black Church to return to its roots by redefining its mission to the world through an "Africentric lens." This worldview grounds the Christian faith in a particular expression of the Gospel from the vantage of the oppressed – in Baltimore or Johannesburg,

---

[87] William J. Walls, *The African Methodist Episcopal Zion Church: Reality of the Black Church* (Charlotte: A.M.E. Zion Publishing House, 1974), 22.

in Chicago or Freetown – and connects its practice in the mission of liberation of all people. For Wilmore, Africentrism is not merely:

> ...defining everything in the world in terms of what Native Africans have done, thought, or believed; it is equally focused on the history and culture of African Americans. Nor is it total rejection of the value of European, Euro-American, or any other civilization. It is not an anti-white version of black nationalism. Africentrism is rather a studied openness to the knowledge, wisdom, and spirituality of African and the African diaspora, and the willingness, on the strength of that acquirement, to always ask the question, "What does this datum of insight, knowledge, or experience have to do with the suppression of truth about black people and the oppression of the black world, and to what extent will it detract from or enhance liberation, justice and democratic development for Africans, the diaspora, and all poor and oppressed people throughout the world?"[88]

Of course, Africentrism, as a concept is not without criticism. There are many who mistakenly assume that it is simply a "racial" response to European concepts, practices and modes of thinking. It is therefore seen as reactionary and not founded in a legitimate worldview. As Julia Speller points out:

> In the minds of many scholars, black and white, it (Africentrism) is seen as reverse racist, anti-white, culturally chauvinistic, and separatist. Even in local churches, many firmly believe that an emphasis on an Africentric identity is in diametric opposition to an affirmation that upholds an identity in Christ. In an ideal world this would be true. Unfortunately, in light of the continuing struggles of being black in America, there is a need to regain and maintain a positive sense of self and experience a heightened level of individual and communal wholeness that prepares African Americans for engagement in the world as subjects and not objects. Through Africentric lenses, the mandates and commitments of the Christian gospel take on new dimensions. The liberation of African peoples all over the world, for example, ceases to be an exclusive,

---

[88] Gayraud Wilmore, *Pragmatic Spirituality: The Christian Faith through an Africentric Lens* (New York and London: New York University Press, 2004), 11.

ethnically centered goal when seen through Africentric lenses that honor and respect the totality of humanity as a divine expression of God.[89]

Speller insists that more than a reactionary response to Eurocentric culture an ideals, Africentrism can freshly illuminate the Christian Gospel and liberate Africans in the diaspora and all humanity created in the image of God.

Africentric Christianity is an answer to both the academic/ideological system of subjugating African and African American beliefs and practices, and the existential reality of hegemony and oppression (race, class and gender) that is upheld and defended with supposedly Christian arguments, or at least by professed Christians. Since much of this academic blasphemy is either explicitly or implicitly promulgated in seminaries and universities, it is necessary to "reinterpret" African American religious history. Wilmore points out "three unfortunate racist assumptions in some white seminaries and Bible colleges about church history:"[90] The first assumption is that real, honest-to-goodness church history is the history of the mainstream white denominations and their European antecedents. Real church history, in other words, is white church history. The second assumption is that any serious religious beliefs among blacks must have begun with the Portuguese attempt to Christianize the coasts of Africa from the last quarter of the fifteenth century. The third assumption has been that African American church history, if one concedes that such a discipline does exist, is practically and morally dysfunctional inasmuch as it tends to preserve and encourage the continuing disunity of the One, Holy, Catholic, and Apostolic Church of Christ.[91] These assumptions point out some of the "logical" arguments presented by cynics and critics of Africentricism who see it as superfluous and irrelevant to the Christian faith, not to mention the aims of liberation and social justice. As a matter of course, Wilmore presents three areas of "reinterpretation" of church history in pursuit of a "pragmatic spirituality":

> (1.) The priority of the contact of both Judaism and Christianity with African people, and the recognition of the African continent as the appropriate place to begin a comprehensive chronology of African

---

89 Julia M. Speller, *Walkin' the Talk: Keepin' the Faith in Africentric Congregations* (Cleveland: The Pilgrim Press, 2005), xxiv.
90 Ibid., 28.
91 Ibid., 28-30.

American religion... (2.) Research focusing on the nature and function of slave religion, its continuity with the African past, and the significant role of the African American churches founded during those days and their continuation in the long struggle for racial advancement... (3.) Challenging the assumption that the religious experience of African Americans is only a little eddy gurgling in the marshlands alongside the great rushing stream of American Christianity.[92]

To be sure, a reinterpretation of Black Church history in these terms, in the context of African American history, will invaluably assist in the all-important task of engendering a healthy self-concept in the face of debilitating realities of injustice and inequality in African American communities.

Institutional, economic and environmental racism gravely affect Black life in inner cities, especially psychologically. An Africentric consciousness goes a long way in boosting personal and collective self-esteem for African Americans. A sense of self-pride and self-determination of African Americans has militated against the effects of racial oppression and injustice. This is one of the positive effects of the enduring communal ethos often credited to the Black Church. It can be traced to an "African spirituality" that defines the bonds of family and community and withstands threats to unity and stability. This spirituality is expressed in, but not limited to, the African American Church. As Christian social ethicist Peter Paris notes:

> The 'spirituality' of a people refers to the animating and integrative power that constitutes the principal frame of meaning for individual and collective experiences. Metaphorically, the spirituality of a people is synonymous with the soul of a people: the integrating center of their power and meaning. In contrast with that of some peoples, however, African spirituality is never disembodied but always integrally connected with the dynamic movement of life. On the one hand, the goal of that movement is the struggle for survival while, on the other hand, it is the union of those forces of life that the power either to threaten and destroy life, one the one hand, or to preserve and enhance it, on the other hand.[93]

---

[92] Ibid., 32-38.
[93] Peter J. Paris, *The Spirituality of African Peoples: The Search for a Common Moral Discourse* (Minneapolis: Fortress Press, 1995), 22.

The mission of transforming African American communities in inner cities must involve recapturing our African spirituality in a contemporary context. This is a two-fold venture. On the one-hand it involves *reconciling* the rupturing relationship between the Black Church and the Black community. On the other hand it involves *restoring* a sense of "communality" that is central to African and African American identity. Reconciliation must first involve acknowledgement of a fault and/or violation of the relationship before forgiveness and resolution can occur. In this sense, the Black Church can be prophetic in calling out the "sin" of its own negligence and apathy toward the suffering of the Black Community, as well as assess the historical, political, and economic forces that have directly and indirectly damaged Black neighborhoods. The Black Church can also be priestly in bringing about healing and reconciliation by extending compassion and concern for the well-being of the victimized and the vulnerable.

The bridge between the divide that appears to exist between the Black Church and the African American community must begin with the recovery of African communality, which is central to Africentric Christianity. As Lee Butler asserts, "Most Africans think first and foremost in terms of the good of the group, that is, the community. They secondly think of themselves, but only as individuals related to a group."[94] Butler goes on to describe the interrelatedness of all things in African communality. The highest community value is cooperation. Even one's sense of self is related to a collective self. "An individual life is given meaning only within the context of the life of the whole community."[95] Every action of the individual has consequences for the entire community. These actions and consequences, in African communality, are all a part of the sacred world. This is very different, if not diametrically opposed, to the Western worldview that separates and demarcates between the sacred and the secular. Butler also bemoans the prophetic shift that occurred in the Black Church as a result of the separation between social action and spirituality. She states:

> One of the leading paradigms of Western culture has been the separation of the sacred and the secular. Unfortunately, African America, as a culture

---

[94] Lee Butler, *A Loving Home: Caring for African American Marriages and Families* (Cleveland, Ohio: The Pilgrim Press, 2000), 48.
[95] Ibid., 50.

of the West, has also succumbed to this splitting practice of the West. There was a time when it was clearly understood that the church did not simply have its finger on the pulse of the community; rather, the church was the pulsating life-force of the community! Yet somewhere in our history our spirituality transgressed into a segregated worldview by splitting religiosity from social action. It seems we have broken continuity with African spirituality and declared there *is* a separation between the sacred and secular. Delilah discovered our strength in our thick hair of communality and shaved it from our heads.

She rightly notes that the separation between social action and spirituality has resulted in marginalization and alienation:

What was once conceived as a unified whole has been separated into the split personalities of 'church' and 'community.' One of the results of that separation has been a marginalization of the church, which has increased human alienation. The church has traditionally been the place that helped us to find rest from wandering. In it, we have been able to find home. It has been our place to find acceptance, respect, and family. If the church is pushed to the margins, then the possibility of our finding an end to our wandering is decreased. Human alienation and homelessness are increased if the church remains separate from the community.[96]

Wilmore, like Butler, expounds on the notion of social action and spirituality and the Black Church's struggle to maintain this historical nexus. In the context of African communality, which was transported across the Atlantic in the minds and hearts of our African forbears, the Black Church inherited and propagated what Wilmore refers to as a three-fold strategy for the African American community – survival, elevation and liberation.[97] These three motifs were performed both successively and simultaneously throughout the history of the Black community. He states:

Throughout their history African American churches have struggled to maintain a precarious balance between racial advancement on the secular front and winning souls on the Christian evangelism front. This has enabled African American churches to achieve three goals: first, to

---

[96] Ibid., 64.
[97] Wilmore, *Pragmatic Spirituality*, 45-59.

help individuals survive by enabling them, by amazing grace, to subsist in the face of atrocities of white racism; second, to help the race free itself from legal slavery, economic exploitation, and the curse of second-class citizenship; and, third, to elevate the masses, particularly young people, to a level of moral and spiritual integrity through the kind of education in church and school that ennobled the individual and collective life of black people.[98]

The search for a Holy Common Ground for the Black Church and Black community can be rooted in three interrelated concepts that are useful for both parties: African spirituality, Africentric Christianity and Black Liberation Theology. This paper will explore later the concepts more fully within the context of Biblical interpretation, historical analysis, and theological discourse. In order to reconcile the relationship and restore the communal order, a common language must be re-established and an ancient value system must be recovered and re-appropriated. There exist today a few models of "Africentric congregations" which have succeeded in being authentically African-centered in identity and ideology, especially in their sense of responsibility to the African American community. They have achieved this, for the most part, by incorporating and appropriating the Nguzo Saba or Seven Principles of Kwanzaa. Kwanzaa is an African American "holiday that ritually celebrates the African family, community, and culture and serves as a fundamental way of reinforcing the bond between African peoples."[99] The principles can be universally applied as values upon which an entire system of living, relating and acting can be instituted for communal life. They form the basis of a holy common ground upon which to re-build and restore a holy, holistic and healthy community.

From the perspective of the African American Church, the Nguzo Saba can be integrated as ideological and practical markers of responsible and responsive Africentric congregations. Julia Speller uses the principles as a method of mutually connecting faith and culture. While Faith is one of the seven principles, Speller relocates Faith as the foundation of the other six. Faith is not mere intellectual ascent or moral affirmation. Faith is grounded in progressive action and liberating praxis. Speller states, "Within the context

---
98 Ibid., 58.
99 Speller, 7.

of African American Christian congregations…it is imperative that Faith as a foundational principle is explicitly connected to a liberating theology whose hope is in the transforming power of Christ."[100] Furthermore, Speller redefines the seven values. The first is value is Unity (Umoja). It is redefined as the effort to seek and maintain unity that begins with our relationship with God. It affirms our connection to Africa and the Diaspora, and calls forth solidarity among and liberation for all of God's people. The next principle is Self-Determination (Kujichagulia). It is redefined as the ability to define ourselves as daughters and sons of Africa, created in the image of God, and willing to participate in the liberation of those in the Diaspora and the world. Collective Work and Responsibility (Ujima) is to build and maintain our communities as Africans in the Diaspora who live in a context of service and mutual accountability in America and the world, strengthened by the liberating spirit of God. Cooperative Economics (Ujamaa) is to believe in and demonstrate a holistic, multidimensional stewardship that values all our resources, including material, human, intellectual, and spiritual, as gifts to us from God to be developed and used in African American communities, the Diaspora, and the world for the good of all people. Purpose (Nia) is to build and develop our communities in ways that acknowledge the sacredness of our collective work of liberation in the Diaspora, and the world and our dependence on God's power and grace to perform it. Creativity (Kuumba) grounds our creative energy in a renewed and renewing relationship with God that restores African American communities and creates new possibilities for commitment to the Diaspora and the world for the benefit of all people. Finally, Faith (Imani) means to always look to and depend upon the presence and power of the reconciling and liberating spirit of God that transcends what we say, do, think, and dream beyond our imagination for the benefit of all creation. These principles will inform and inspire a vision for a renewed faith community and restored society. At the center of this Africentric Christianity is the liberating power of the Gospel of Jesus Christ. This Gospel has the power to reconcile relationships and restore communities.

    An Africentric conscious congregation is deeply rooted in the community in which it is situated, while being connected to a wider community of the African Diaspora, as well as the global community. Black Churches that are

---
100 Ibid., 8.

relevant and effective in African American communities see themselves as part and parcel of the aforementioned communities, especially in urban neighborhoods. Robert C. Linthicum describes three different views that churches of any ethnicity can have in relation to the city. One view is the Church *in* the city. This church does not feel any particular attachment to that city or identify with the community. "It is simply physically present in that community."[101] The second view is the Church *to* the city and *to* the community. In its self-interest the Church realizes that if it is going to exist and survive, it must provide services to the community, such as evangelism and social action. Although its concern is commendable, the flaw in this approach is that the Church makes the sole decision of what is best for the community, better known as paternalism. The third view, which is the most powerful and relevant, is that of the Church *with* the community. Linthicum reveals:

> There is a profound difference between being a church *in* or *to* an urban neighborhood, and being a church *with* its neighborhood. When a church takes this third approach, that church incarnates itself in that community. That church becomes flesh of the peoples' flesh and bone of the peoples' bone. It enters into the life of the community and becomes partners with the community in addressing the community's need. That means the church allows people of the community to instruct it as it identifies with the people. It respects those people and perceives them as being people of great wisdom and potential. Such a church joins with the people in dealing with the issues that the people have identified as their own. That is the approach in which the most authentic urban ministry is actually done.[102]

Of course, this view by Linthicum and many other purveyors of community-based ministry models serves to highlight the split between the Church and Community, the sacred and the secular. This phenomenon was once foreign to African American churches, which were always organically and authentically connected to African American communities. However, the effect of assimilation in American culture has led to this detachment. An

---

[101] Robert C. Linthicum, *Empower the Poor: Community Organizing Among the City's 'Rag, Tag and Bobtail,'* (Monrovia, California: MARC/World Vision, 1991), 21.
[102] Ibid., 23.

Africentric Church is a Church *with* community, while realizing its historic and spiritual character. African theologian John Mbiti insists:

> To be human is to belong to the whole community, and to do so involves participating in the beliefs, ceremonies, rituals and festivals of that community. A person cannot detach himself from the religion of his group, for to do so is to be severed from his roots, his foundation, his context of security, his kinships and the entire group of those who make him aware of his own existence. To be without one of these corporate elements is to be out of the whole picture. Therefore, to be without religion amounts to a self-excommunication from the entire life of society, and African peoples do not know how to exist without religion.[103]

Since there is a religious thread of being running through the veins of African Americans, reconciliation between the Black Church and the African American community should not be a daunting task. The challenge is not getting the Church or the community to be more religious; the issue is getting both to be more spiritually and morally responsible to the claims of the Gospel to bring "good news to the poor" and to "set at liberty those who are captive."

Many African American Churches have realized the inextricable connection between the well-being of the community and the vitality of the congregation. They have embraced a mission of community outreach that is more than a "hand-out" but a "hand-up." Christian community development in the African American context has become a preferred method of neighborhood revitalization. Nile Harper points out that these churches have moved beyond charity to true social justice:

> With this focus on community-building, many churches in city centers are taking leadership in creative ministries of redevelopment. This is especially visible in a number of African American churches, which have gone far beyond providing a safety net of social service. They are rebuilding whole urban communities, creating affordable housing, developing employment, providing community health care, and establishing good-quality schools. What begins as isolated acts of charity, individual actions of compassion, or programs of social service can develop under the power of God's spirit through creative leadership into

---
[103] John S. Mbiti, *African Religions and Philosophy* (Portsmouth, NH: Heinemann, 1999), 2.

very positive collaborative actions for systemic justice, which changes policy and structure that have oppressed people.[104]

As such, an African-centered spirituality provides the foundation for authentic, organic and mutual community. Drawing from the rich reservoir of African communality, churches are able to become responsible "stewards" of the commonwealth bequeathed to them by God. The Kwanzaa principle of *Cooperative Economics* provides grounding for community development. As Speller corroborates, "Cooperative Economics is to believe in and demonstrate a holistic, multidimensional stewardship that values all our resources, including material, human, intellectual, and spiritual resources as gifts from God to be developed and used in African American communities, the Diaspora, and the world for the good of all people."[105] A theological and spiritual understanding of community focuses the Church on sharing its resources in order to maximize the combined assets of its collaborative entities. Speller goes on to say:

> Viewing material, human, intellectual, and spiritual resources as gifts from God shifts the perception of obligation from profits for the community to good stewardship for God. When this obligation is centered on one's community alone it runs the risk of selective distribution and opens the way for exploitation as the rich get richer and the poor remain poor. When the obligation is centered on the Divine, however, it is empowered by a different source. There is a celebration and cultivation of gifts beyond the material, creating a more holistic notion of Cooperative Economics, shifting the emphasis from profit to stewardship.[106]

Speller has played a significant role in one of the best examples of a transformative Africentric congregation, the Trinity United Church of Christ in Chicago, pastored by the Reverend Dr. Otis Moss III. This congregation became "Unashamedly Black and unapologetically Christian" under the extraordinary leadership of the Reverend Dr. Jeremiah A. Wright, Jr., the same prophetic personality that was unfairly vilified as the pastor who nearly derailed the candidacy of President Barack Obama. It is clear that Mr. Obama was drawn to the spirit and mission of Trinity Church and its pastor. Trinity and Dr. Wright

---

104 Nile Harper, *Vital Signs in Urban Churches* (Eugene, Oregon: Wipf & Stock, 1999), 5.
105 Speller, 70.
106 Andrew Billingsley, *Mighty Like a River: The Black Church and Social Reform* (New York: Oxford University Press, 1999), 71.

proved being culturally relevant and socially and politically active would not be a deterrent to church growth. Andrew Billingsley records:

> Afrocentricity seemed to be a major factor enhancing the phenomenal growth of the church. Within 11 years after Wright's appointment as pastor, the membership of Trinity United had grown from 87 members to more than 4,000 members! Such phenomenal growth, along with the Black Value System, catapulted Trinity and Wright into the forefront of national leadership. By 1996, with more than 4,500 members, Trinity was the largest congregation in the United Church of Christ denomination, still a largely white organization. Moreover, the church completed a new $14 million building only discover that it still has to conduct three Sunday services. All of these factors bear strong testimony to the viability of this church even as it seeks to successfully integrate its Christian heritage with its African American heritage.[107]

Billingsley quotes Dr. Wright's reflections upon the Trinity experience in teaching and living an Africentric curriculum:

> The pastor says, "For 17 years we have been trying to do Christian education from the black perspective...We have used the curriculum put together by Reverend Barbara Allen and Dr. Yvonne Delk. We have used the curriculum put together by our former assistant direct of Christian Education, (Dr.) Julia Speller; and now we are using the curriculum being developed by Dr. Colleen Birchett. It combines the Afrocentric and Christocentric perspective or foci, giving our young people a weekly infusion of the Bible and a weekly infusion of African American perspectives on biblical themes. It is based on Nguzo Saba, the seven principles of Kwanzaa developed by Maulama Karenga: unity, self-determination, collective work and responsibility, cooperative economics, purpose, creativity, and faith.[108]

After establishing a commitment to its motto, "Unashamedly Black and unapologetically Christian," in creed and deed, the Trinity Church adopted a "Black Value System" which had ten elements:

---
107 Ibid., 181.
108 Ibid., 180.

1. Commitment to God
2. Commitment to the Black Community
3. Commitment to the Black Family
4. Dedication to the Pursuit of Education
5. Dedication to the Pursuit of Excellence
6. Adherence to the Black Work Ethic
7. Commitment to Self-Discipline and Self-Respect
8. Disavowal of the Pursuit of Middle-classness
9. Pledges of Community Spirit
10. Personal Commitment to the Black Value System[109]

This Black Value System is based upon the African value system known as Maat. Asa G. Hilliard describes Maat in relation to the African world view:

> An African worldview is derived from deep study of everything in the environment, including the weather, stars, animals, agriculture, and each other. At the end of that study of the environment, almost all Africans believe that God has given us a book, and the thing that we study is that book. And, if we study it hard enough, God's principles and values will be revealed in what we see. Out of that the core principle that permeates the worldview of Africans—even though they have different names for it and different places—is a value system that sums up in one word everything that they have learned. That value system is called Maat. In some places, they call it mojo, which is where we get the phrase: 'I've got my mojo working.' (Unfortunately, we're so uninformed about who we are that we don't even know the origin of the words we use.) Maat is one of the highest statements of an ancient African value system. It takes seven English words to sum up Maat: truth, justice, order, harmony, balance, reciprocity, and righteousness. You don't study Maat; you must be Maat.[110]

Of course, there are Black Churches doing impressive community development and empowerment that are not as explicitly as Africentric as Trinity United Church of Christ. However, it can said that these churches

---
109 Ibid., 172-73.
110 Asa G. Hilliard, "Liberating the Ancient Utterances," in Iva E. Carruthers, Frederick D. Haynes, II, Jeremiah A. Wright, Jr., *Blow the Trumpet in Zion: Global Vision and Action for the 21st Century Black Church* (Philadelphia: Fortress Press, 2005), 66.

harbor and herald an Africentric ethic of communalism and mission to the least, the lost and the left out. One of the most effective agents of community transformation is the Greater Allen A.M.E. Cathedral of Jamaica-Queens, New York, led by former congressman and college president, the Reverend Dr. Floyd Flake. Flake and Allen have "purchased a block-long commercial district in Queens and transformed the dilapidated area into a collection of thriving businesses including legal offices, a restaurant, and a drug store with a total value of 50 million dollars.[111] Pastor Flake sees community development as an important extension of the Church's ministry. He states:

> Community development in many ways constitutes the essence of an extended and successful ministry. After all, ministry results from people who, in following God, change first themselves and then their surroundings. This process entails changing how people think about themselves, their lives, and their relationships. There is no more powerful tool for developing a community than changing the quality of the lives of the people in that community.[112]

Changing "how people think about themselves" is one of the attendant effects of Africentric spirituality. The aim is ultimately liberation and empowerment for persons *in* community.

Most of the credit for outstanding community development by churches goes to pastors. It is true that transformative churches are led by transformative leaders, namely pastors and their staffs and key leaders. However, a pastor cannot lead this brand of prophetic ministry without some buy-in and consensus of prophetic and progressive minded congregations whose transformational approach to ministry illustrate the Gospel in action. Stephen C. Raser and Michael J.N. Dash believe that the Black Church is essentially "ex-centric." That is, they believe that God's intent is for the Church is for it to move beyond its narrow internal focus into world in order to compassionately care for and empower those who are disadvantages and distressed. For that approach to be effective, there must be maximum involvement from the congregation. Raser and Dash insist:

---

[111] Anthony B. Pinn, *The Black Church in the Post-Civil Rights Era* (Maryknoll, New York: Orbis Books, 2002), 77.
[112] Floyd H. Flake, Elaine McCollins Flake and Edwin C. Reed, *African American Church Management Book* (Valley Forge: Judson Press, 2005), 89.

There is need to find ways to maximize participation of individuals and groups in congregations. This commitment becomes meaningful as congregations come to grips with the community among whom their journey is set. They must become critically aware of their community so that their witness is determined by the hard knowledge of concrete realities of the human condition. Congregations must identify with and serve the poor, heal the blind and the sick, and engage in the process of liberating the oppressed.[113]

An Africentric congregation is characterized by responsible, ethical stewardship in relationship with its understandings of God, the Bible and its history. At the heart of Black worship is the reverence for the Word of God. The Church perceives the authority of its mission as found in biblical preaching and teaching. The Black Church becomes a prophetic congregation when it infuses its Africentric spirituality into its mission and ministry and then reflects upon its efficacy toward transformation of itself and the people to whom they have been called to minister. Robert Michael Franklin offers a framework for prophetic or "public ministry" that leads to transformation.[114] It has five phases: Phase One – The Ministry of Charity which is focused on direct, immediate relief of pain and suffering; Phase Two – The Ministry of Transitional Support which is focused upon longer-term but not permanent counseling and assistance that facilitates the journey from dependence to self-sufficiency and self-determination; Phase Three – The Ministry of Social Service which moves beyond providing counseling to providing regular services to the community; Phase Four – The Ministry of Justice which is focused upon representing and/or advocating the needs of the people to the public systems and structures of power; Phase Five – The Ministry of Transformation is evidenced when a congregation becomes a leader or co-leader in crafting a vision of the beloved community and the organizing the capital, mobilizing the people, negotiating the systems, and hammering out the details in order to develop new and better communities.[115]

---

113 Stephen C. Raser and Michael J.N. Dash (*The Mark of Zion: Congregational Life in Black Churches*, Cleveland, Ohio: Pilgrim Press, 2003), 62.
114 Franklin, *Crisis in the Village*, 162.
115 Ibid., 164.

CHAPTER SEVEN
CAN THESE BONES LIVE?: A BIBLICAL VISION FOR RESTORATION OF THE AFRICAN AMERICAN COMMUNITY

The hand of the Lord came upon me and brought me out in the Spirit of the Lord, and set me down in the midst of the valley; and it was full of bones. Then he caused me to pass by them all round, and behold, there were very many in the open valley; and indeed they were very dry. And He said to me, 'Son of man, can these bones live?' So I answered, 'O Lord God, you know."
Ezekiel 37:1-3 (NKJV)

The First Book of the African American community is the Bible. In most instances the Bible is the first book that most African slaves ever heard, saw and learned to memorize, recite and read. It held mystery to Africans for many reasons. Slaves were prohibited by law and custom from reading it for fear that it would "liberate" them. It was the authoritative document of the Christian religion, read, taught and preached from in the white churches they attended. It contained fascinating stories of the vicissitudes and victories of the children of Israel, the soaring oratory of the prophets and kings, and the miraculous accounts of a hero-healer named Jesus. The definitive event of the Old Testament was the Exodus episode, which held a captivating hope for a people experiencing their own brand of existential oppression. Moses and the prophets were the heroes of the drama who were opening acts to the lead actor/hero of the New Testament, Jesus Christ, the great liberator. James H. Evans affirms the centrality of the biblical text to African American identity:

> African-Americans were defined by slaveholders in the nineteenth century as outsiders with reference to the biblical story. In response, African Americans sought to establish their place within the biblical story by identifying with the Israelites – with an emphasis on political freedom – or the Cushites – with an emphasis on cultural integrity. Both of these emphases were supported by their reading of the New Testament, which

confirmed their personal worth in the sight of God. Finding their place meant that the African slaves and their descendants read the Bible as an imaginative text that served the self-revelation of God and as a historical narrative that confirmed God's active presence in human affairs.[116]

The Gospel message is firmly rooted in the Judeo-Christian traditions of redemption, reconciliation and restoration, especially in the direst circumstances. The overarching narrative of the Bible speaks of a sovereign God who seeks the lost, the last and the least in order to restore order to a world fraught with a chaotic conundrum as a consequence of sin – a violation of the natural harmony of creation (shalom). This message is reinforced in vibrant practices which bring the Gospel to life. The history of Israel points to the acts of God to restore justice and peace in a world of violence. After the fall of humans in creation, a cycle of sin and oppression was born that was perpetrated by those who had once been victims. The laws, commandments and codes of the nation of Israel were instituted to honor God and maintain harmony with God, nature and humanity. Justice was spiritual and social, not merely legal or political. Sacred rituals of worship and sacrifice were instituted by priests for restitution and reconciliation. Over time many of those rituals became perfunctory and were not consistent with a life of respect, honor and reverence for God and humanity. It was necessary for God to speak words of correction through the prophets in order to salvage the nation and resume the plan of establishing the Kingdom of God on earth. Pastor Walter Malone describes this biblical-ethical imperative:

> Although the children of Israel were called upon to constitute a new community of faith after their deliverance from bondage in Egypt, they became susceptible to the idolatry of greed, and perpetuated economic injustice against each other. ….. But it was at this moment in history that God sent prophets like Isaiah, Jeremiah, Amos, and Micah to speak against the nation because Israel had become wealthy by op- pressing the poor. Both Isaiah and Amos reminded Israel that God demanded more than formalism and ritualism in worship.

---

[116] James H. Evans, Jr., *We Have Been Believers: An African American Systematic Theology* (Minneapolis: Fortress Press, 1992), 51.

God demands justice for the poor and oppressed, and without this, Israel's worship would not be acceptable....[117]

Both the Old and New Testaments point to a "preferential option for the poor." Codes and customs were enforced to protect and provide for the "least of these." These measures were put in place to ensure balance in the community. The role of the prophets was to remind the nation of its obligation to the widows, poor and orphans. The prophet Isaiah makes a direct correlation between righteous worship and social justice:

Is not this the kind of fasting I have chosen: to loose the chains of injustice and untie the cords of the yoke, to set the oppressed free and break every yoke? Is it not to share your food with the hungry and to provide the poor wanderer with shelter – when you see the naked, to clothe him, and not to turn away from your own flesh and blood? Then your light will break forth like the dawn, and your healing will quickly appear; then your righteousness will go before you, and the glory of the Lord will be your rear guard.[118]

Those concerned about the dis-connect between the Black Church and the African American community will discover that the book of Ezekiel, particularly chapter 37, offers a biblical approach to restoration of community:

The hand of the LORD was on me, and he brought me out by the Spirit of the LORD and set me in the middle of a valley; it was full of bones. He led me back and forth among them, and I saw a great many bones on the floor of the valley, bones that were very dry. He asked me, "Son of man, can these bones live?" I said, "Sovereign LORD, you alone know."

Then he said to me, "Prophesy to these bones and say to them, 'Dry bones, hear the word of the LORD! This is what the Sovereign LORD says to these bones: I will make breath[a] enter you, and you will come to life. I will attach tendons to you and make flesh come upon you and cover you with skin; I will put breath in you, and you will come to life. Then you will know that I am the LORD.'"

---

[117] Walter Malone, Jr., "The Black Church and Community Economic Empowerment through a Community Development Corporation" (D.Min. Thesis, United Theological Seminary, Dayton, Ohio, 1993), 28-29. Also See Isaiah 1:13, 17 and Amos 5:21-24.
[118] Isaiah 58:6-12.

So I prophesied as I was commanded. And as I was prophesying, there was a noise, a rattling sound, and the bones came together, bone to bone. 8 I looked, and tendons and flesh appeared on them and skin covered them, but there was no breath in them.

Then he said to me, "Prophesy to the breath; prophesy, son of man, and say to it, 'This is what the Sovereign LORD says: Come, breath, from the four winds and breathe into these slain, that they may live.'" 10 So I prophesied as he commanded me, and breath entered them; they came to life and stood up on their feet—a vast army.

Then he said to me: "Son of man, these bones are the people of Israel. They say, 'Our bones are dried up and our hope is gone; we are cut off.' 12 Therefore prophesy and say to them: 'This is what the Sovereign LORD says: My people, I am going to open your graves and bring you up from them; I will bring you back to the land of Israel. 13 Then you, my people, will know that I am the LORD, when I open your graves and bring you up from them. 14 I will put my Spirit in you and you will live, and I will settle you in your own land. Then you will know that I the LORD have spoken, and I have done it, declares the LORD.'" [119]

One of the dominant themes for the people of Israel is restoration – spiritual, physical and moral. And one of the most dramatic portrayals of that theme is the narrative of the prophet Ezekiel in the Valley of Dry Bones, found in chapter 37. Ezekiel himself was an extraordinary individual. A mystic with a vision, he was able to utilize channels of communication not normally available to others. Like prophets before him, Ezekiel was called to bring a message of repentance and obedience to divine will upon the Israelites. Unlike Jeremiah and Isaiah, Ezekiel's emphasis is not judgment, but on comforting. From an ancient concentration camp near Babylon, Ezekiel writes his prophecies to encourage the Jewish exiles.

Ezekiel was a younger contemporary of the prophet Jeremiah. His prophetic mission is to warn the "house of Israel" of pending ruin. He preaches his message to Judah and Jerusalem, making known Jerusalem's abominations.[120] After the fall of Jerusalem and Judah the messages of comfort in chapters 34-48 are addressed to Jews scattered all over the world rather than

---
119   Ezekiel 37:1-14.
120   Ezekiel 16:2; 22:2

specifically to those newly exiled in Babylonia.[121] Ezekiel was a man of the people, who despite his priestly descent was well acquainted with the social, economic, political and religious aspects of Judah's life. The book of Ezekiel contains four visions: the glory in the storm cloud (Chapters 1-3), the eating of a scroll held in Yahweh's hand (Chapter 2:8 – Chapter 3:3), the coming destruction of Jerusalem (Chapter 9); and the resurrection of the nation (Chapter 37:1-14). The latter is a biblical paradigm for community reconciliation and restoration. Ezekiel's preaching connects holiness to moral responsibility and communal accountability just as the bones are miraculously linked one to another. This miracle gives Israel hope of divine renewal manifested in national restoration. Roland Harrison states:

> Earlier prophets had proclaimed that the very concept of divine holiness demanded the rejection of rebellious Israel, if only for a short period. Ezekiel, however, argued conversely that this same holiness rendered the ultimate restoration of the nation inevitable, since divine honor was bound up with the destiny of Israel. The promise of restoration itself constituted an act of divine grace which would lead to repentance on the part of the faithful minority among the exiles (Ezekiel 36:16ff). With an act of cleansing and the creation of a new spiritual attitude of mind, the process of regeneration would commence in earnest. Only then could the dry bones of Israel (Ezekiel 37:1ff), horribly and helplessly abandoned heretofore, become clothed with flesh through the action of the divine spirit and live, quickened to a regenerate life.[122]

This story is one of the most mystifying texts of the Judeo-Christian Canon and yet one of most captivating stories in the African American preaching tradition. In a modern context, Ezekiel can be seen as a minister called to serve in the Valley of Dry Bones. Many of the neighborhoods of Black communities seem like a Valley of Dry Bones. There is dearth, destruction, depression, death and desolation. There is seen the remains of a once vibrant community and the shadow of a formerly overachieving people who have moved "up from slavery" and de jure segregation. We often lament this reality,

---
121 Charles M. Laymon, ed., *The Interpreter's One-Volume Commentary on the Bible* (Nashville: Abingdon Press, 1989), 411.
122 Roland Kenneth Harrison, *Introduction to the Old Testament* (Peobody, Massachusetts: Prince Press, 1999), 853.

but seldom address it with relevant, liberating ministries and programs that seek to transform the conditions. In the A.M.E. Zion Church, as in many denominational conferences, on an annual basis, we give something called "the State of the Church" and "the State of the Country" reports. We often cite the problems, plagues, and predicaments of the African American Church in general and our denomination in particular, while sometimes listing some recommendations for action. Nonetheless, rarely do we ever follow up with concrete, measurable strategies for implementation and transformation. This is an ongoing challenge for the Church – long on rhetoric and short on execution.

Ezekiel was appointed by his "Bishop" to a valley where the bones were very dry. This suggests something about the bones and the state of the valley. This is a long standing problem that has endured more than one generation. Notice that Ezekiel was not instructed to analyze the bones, or assess the bones, or account for the bones. He was instructed to ADDRESS the bones. God sensitizes the prophet by sending him to the Valley. He does not do it to pique his curiosity but to prick his conscience. You do not have anything to SAY if you have not had anything to SEE. We may not have realized it lately, but our church is in the Valley. We have done the analysis; now we must act.

I am sure Ezekiel wanted to ask some questions: How did these bones die? How did they end up like this? How did they end up here? Who let this happen to these bones? Is anyone accountable to these bones? Did anyone care about these bones?

God gives a rejoinder to Ezekiel internal inquiries. It becomes clear that the restoration of the nation and the resurrection of the people are contingent upon the connection of holy people with the Holy Spirit. The key to transforming our decimated conclaves of dry bones is a life-transforming experience with the power of the Holy Spirit. That Spirit in turn will lead us to speak a Word of New Life. Although it looks dire, drear, and dry we still have an obligation to say something to the bones. Relevant proclamation is contingent upon proximity and sensitivity, which leads to receptivity and connectivity. There is a troubling correlation between our religious fervor and social apathy. Dr. Martin Luther King once said, "Any religion that professes to be concerned about the soul, but is unconcerned about the conditions that damage the soul is a dry-as-dust religion."

In this text we can perceive these dry bones in three ways: First, they are *Dead Bones*. They are spiritually lifeless because they have become disconnected from their life source. They are isolated from the spiritual reservoirs that once nourished them, like the rich religious oases of the Temple community. Secondly, they are *Despondent and Dejected Bones*. They have suffered so much loss that they have given up hope of ever returning to the Promised Land of abundance and prosperity. Their community has been systemically underdeveloped and disenfranchised for so long that they've given up hope of ever being revived. Thirdly, they are *Disassembled and Dispersed Bones*. They have been torn asunder as a community. Their families have deteriorated. Their kinship ties are dwindling. Their neighborly ties are diminishing. Instead of being members of the expansive Diaspora they have become remote, distant clusters of disconnected bodies. They are disengaged from each other, from God, from community and the Church. Isolation and separation has become normal and acceptable.

Miraculously, God has sent a hopeful messenger with a healing message. There is Good News. Ezekiel's message is bi-directional. He speaks to the bones and to the wind. He calls forth the people and the Spirit. God has given Ezekiel something to say because God has given him something to see. As the Church of Jesus Christ, and as proclaimers of the Gospel, the Good News, God is calling us to say something. Based on the experience of the prophet Ezekiel, there are three interrelated ways that the Church can say something.

God places Ezekiel in an unsettling and disconcerting place – a Valley full of bones. The prophet views the setting in the context of one piercing question, "Can these bones live?" In the perspective of the prophet it does not look promising. But through the eyes of faith there is a glimmer of hope. This hope can only be found in the God who placed him in the Valley. The only response that a man of faith can give is "Lord, only you know if new life is possible in this situation!" Dr. Gardner C. Taylor examines the question:

> Before that kind of awesome question, with the very breath of God felt upon his spirit, the preacher dare not rush forth babbling bland assurances and mouthing easy answers. The preacher knows that when he or she gazes at the valley of dry bones, something deep within suggests that death is death and that is that, world without end. A quick and easy yes

is more than half a lie, for the preacher cannot help having doubts. On the other had if he or she surrenders to the doubt and says, "No, these bones cannot live," the preacher impeaches the power of the eternal God. Thus ought there to be some central hush in the preacher's utterance, for he or she stands in the midst of life-and-death matters, with God very much in the midst of it all.[123]

Here Taylor emphasizes the importance of careful response in the face of disconcerting circumstances.

Like Ezekiel, we may not be able to see much hope with our naked eyes. The situation looks very bleak when we look at the condition of our African American community. There are gangs and drugs and boarded up houses. Our government is unresponsive. Our schools are failing our children. Our families are barely holding it together. Our financial institutions are crumbling. Our housing stock is eroding. We are forced to face the query, "Can these bones live?" Rather than excuses, we can offer an exception to the rule. Our ancestors always knew that "There's a bright side somewhere." There is hope when God is present. However, we must use spiritual eyes of discernment to see God in the midst of a valley that has been painted by the media and the naysayers who have never spent much time in the Valley. When we look around we can see the potential more than we can see the problem. We can find leaders who will be accountable. We can find people that have defied the odds and have kept their faith and their families together. We can find financial partners who will invest in neighborhoods that hold the key to a renaissance of an entire city. We can find plenty of solid housing properties that can be restored and empty lots that can be rebuilt to form a new village community in the midst of the Valley.

Ezekiel is a prophet with a pastor's heart. He reviews the setting and begins to see what God sees. The people are worth serving in word and deed. They are not to be preached at, but to be preached to. The message is filled with hope in spite of the hell they are currently experiencing.

Ezekiel is sensitized to the plight of the bones while he is placed in the setting of the Valley. Being sensitized leads him to give the proper response to the bones. He does not treat them as means to an end. They are not a statistic. They are not a problem to be solved. They are people with potential. He does

---

[123] Gardner C. Taylor, *"The Foolishness of Preaching,"* *The Lyman Beecher Lecture Series* (1976) at Yale University, in *The Words of Gardner Taylor, Volume 5* (Valley Forge: Judson Press, 2001), 169.

not give the pat response as if these bones were the usual suspects. He does not judge the bones by saying, "These bones probably got what they deserved." He does not further stigmatize or marginalize the bones by saying, "These bones belong here in the Valley so they cannot bother those of us who have made up to the house on the hill." He does not respond paternalistically by saying, "These bones sure are pitiful and helpless. They would not be able to be anything without me. They need my help in order to fulfill their potential because I am better than them."

The proper response of one who has been sent to help is to serve the bones as a priestly obligation. As Africans in American, and as members of a community of mutuality, we must respond with mutual respect and love for the people we have been sent to serve. When people are facing death they do not need to be reminded that they are dying. They need a word of hope that defies death. They need someone to tell them that they can defeat death through the power of the Holy Spirit. That is what resurrection is all about. The bones got up because they heard a Word that resisted and transcended their Valley existence. The ministry of encouragement will always bring restoration and regeneration in the face of extinction and annihilation. The ministry of genuine caring persons will cause a renaissance in a valley that has been neglected and abandoned. What looked like a haunting carcass will be miraculously transformed into a vibrant, vigorous and vivacious human being.

Ezekiel's message and ministry resulted in a miracle. The bones came together and formed the likeness of a reconstructed body. They now looked like they did before their ranks were decimated. But the appearance of cohesion was not enough. There was something invisible that was indispensable to their resurgence. They needed a return to their source – the Spirit of God. This was the source they first encountered in Africa. Ezekiel must have remembered the ancient story of the Creation from the book of Genesis, adapted from the Egyptian Book of the Dead. The narrative says that the first man had the form of being, but did not become a living soul until God breathed into him the breath of life. Likewise, the Spirit of God and the spirit of ancestors began to inhabit these resurrected bones. The bones not only heard Ezekiel's message they were changed by what they heard. They looked at themselves differently now. They saw a solution and it was within their grasp.

One implication of Ezekiel's response that benefits our communities is that the valleys in our Black neighborhoods will never be changed unless they are confronted. The conditions that create valleys must be confronted and challenged. Prophets must be willing to engage the powers that be. There are forces that must be met head on with the message of social justice. Someone must be willing to speak truth to power at the same time that they preach power to the people. This is the missing component in many of ministries in that many churches are valleys that collect dry bones instead of Spirit-filled houses of liberation. The bones might do a lot of rattling, making a lot of noise, and even come together. Our dry bones have been aggregated and assimilated, but they have not been activated. They have "the form of godliness, but are denying the power thereof." We must call on the Spirit to motivate these bones to action. The Spirit can bring the bones together in order to work in synch as "an exceedingly great army." A new legion of soldiers will come to life to rebuild and restore the Valley into a new Promised Land. An army is certainly needed to build the community. Just as the children of Israel had to overcome adversaries and ward off enemies in order to possess the Promised Land, a new generation of potential dwellers of the "land of milk and honey" will have to fight for the future by possessing, protecting and preserving the new Promised Land.

CHAPTER EIGHT
THE BEAUTIFUL CITY OF GOD: A NEW HOLY COMMON GROUND

They devoted themselves to the apostles' teaching and to fellowship, to the breaking of bread and to prayer. Everyone was filled with awe at the many wonders and signs performed by the apostles. All the believers were together and had everything in common. They sold property and possessions to give to anyone who had need. Every day they continued to meet together in the temple courts. They broke bread in their homes and ate together with glad and sincere hearts, praising God and enjoying the favor of all the people. And the Lord added to their number daily those who were being saved.[124]

Acts 2:42-47

The Ezekiel passage explicitly highlights that through the spoken Word and the empowering of the Spirit, a dry community comes to life. Similarly, the book of Acts illustrates the dramatic beginning of a new alternative community known as the Church. The followers of Jesus Christ were faithful to the directive of their martyred leader and Lord. They assembled in the Upper Room to wait for the arrival of their promise of power. Luke's eyewitness account of the Acts of the Apostles begins with the phenomenal acts of the Holy Spirit. Precipitated by fervent, concerted prayer, the miraculous move of the Holy Spirit is the fulfillment of the hope and prayer of Jesus Christ, if only for a unique moment in time, "Lord make us one."

Their unity is characterized first by the convergence of their diversity. They were assembled together in one place on one accord, itself quite remarkable given the many different ethnic groups represented in that assembly. Upon receiving the outpour of the Holy Spirit they were able to communicate with one another in their own tongues. Peter's sermon, based on the book of the prophet Joel, references the multi-generational and multi-gender promise of God to "pour out His Spirit on all flesh. Sons and daughters will prophesy…

---
[124] Acts 2:42-47.

your young men will see visions, your old men will dream dreams. Even on my servants, both men and women, I will pour out my Spirit in those days, and they will prophesy" (vv. 17-18). The response to his preaching was incredible; around three thousand souls were converted and became members of this new community. They became the realization of the prophetic proclamation that pointed to a yet-to-be-seen "Beloved Community."

This text gives a more holistic understanding of a true Pentecostal community. While the so-called charismatic gift of speaking in new tongues toward a divine being gets most of the "miracle mention," perhaps the most remarkable aspect of this cataclysmic event is the new means of relating to other human beings. There is a spontaneous outbreak of *agape* love. The signs and wonders that accompany the miracle are the passionate practices of continuing in: the apostles' doctrine, fellowship, breaking of bread and prayers. These spiritual disciplines are understood in today's post-modern, post-Pentecostal community as fairly regular practices of devotees. The most extraordinary behavior then follows – they held all things in *common*. "So mightily was the love of God shed abroad in their hearts that they did not look upon their material possessions as their own."[125] This is a deliberate statement about the priorities of this new community. New Testament scholar Craig S. Keener says:

> The Greek language Luke uses here is language that Pythagoreans and others used the ideal, utopian community. Those who have argued that the early church made a mistake in (these verses) are thus reading their own views into the Bible, not hearing Luke's message, because Luke portrays this radical lifestyle as the result of the outpouring of the Spirit.[126]

This narrative gives sanguinity to the spiritual pursuit of a new Promised Land. The Holy Spirit gives a new perspective to human relationships and the re-ordering of systems of economic arrangements. The Holy Spirit renews thinking about personal possessions and common wealth. The Holy Spirit reshapes our landscape and reframes our territories into a "Holy Common Ground."

As disciples of Jesus Christ we are called to live out the spiritual disciplines and the radical lifestyles of the first century Christian community. They were

---

125 William MacDonald, *The Believers Bible Commentary* (Nashville: Thomas Nelson Publishers, 1995), 1589.
126 Craig S. Keener, *The IVP Bible Background Commentary New Testament* (Downers Grove, Illinois: InterVarsity Press, 1993), 330.

counter cultural as a minority movement. This parallels the experience of African Americans who were under threat of persecution, terrorization and extermination. They found strength in the faith of their forbears who had "come this far by faith." Like the early disciples, they found it necessary to share all things in common in a system of equality and mutual aid and cooperation. The Acts Two Church gives us the paradigm for a "Holy Common Ground."

The members of the new Church were remaining steadfast in the apostles' doctrine. The apostles had been taught a new code of ethics: Love the Lord your God with all your heart, all your mind, all your soul and all your strength...and love your *neighbor* as you love yourself. They had to reassess what was important now. It was no longer about retaliation, retribution and recrimination. Their priorities were now about reconciliation and restoration. They were no longer to be competitive but to be collaborative. We must reassess our priorities in light of the gospel and the gift of the Holy Spirit.

As African Americans, we sorely need to reassess our priorities. We have been influenced by American individualism and consumerism. We have adopted me-first attitudes that have adversely affected us and our communities; the Gospel compels us to love our neighbor as we love ourselves. Self-centeredness is a major threat to community. A key African ideal is summed up in the saying, "I am because we are. And since we are, therefore, I am." Dr. King would say it this way, "I am not all that I can be until you are all that you can be." Our values have become warped.

The good news is that the Holy Spirit has the power to reorient our values. Once the Spirit is poured out on all flesh, we will begin to see our mutual responsibility for our community. We will begin to envision a new Promised Land that includes all of God's children. We gain access to God through the Spirit which, in turn, empowers us to change ourselves and the conditions that would imprison and impede us. Our service to one another becomes an extension of our worship of God. As Robert Michael Franklin asserts:

> For black churches, access to God is provided through the Holy Spirit. The spirit realm is conceived as one of freedom. Slaves who were shackled could experience a bit of absolute freedom by abandoning themselves to God's spirit. Through the careful coordination of visual, audio, olfactory, and tactile stimuli, good worship becomes a form of spiritual therapy

in which human wholeness is actualized through communion with God. God is felt and known through worship that engages the senses. Authentic worship is, in Paul Tillich's terms, a "theonomous" encounter in which participants may relate to God who abhors dichotomies and who reconciles the rational and emotional dimensions of human being, the sacred and the secular, right brain and left, the yin and the yang.[127]

The Holy Spirit provides access to God and undergirds community; hence, the Beloved Community that Dr. King talked about is related to the New Testament movement precipitated by Pentecost. It also has its roots in the Paradise of Adam and Eve and the Promised Land of Moses of Joshua. We must envision a community with proper and perfecting relationships with God, others, and resources (human and material.) Paradise can be "conjured" through the reestablishment of right relationships. Phil Reed describes the principles of Christian Community development in this way:

> As we return to God's perfect plan for his creation in Paradise, we find that not only did Adam and Eve have a relationship with God, but they also had a relationship with each other. The second chapter of Genesis closes with a wedding picture of Adam and Eve standing before God to become "one flesh." In Matthew 19, Jesus refers to this created order to speak about the sacredness of the marriage bond: "What God has joined together, let man not separate" (v.6). In Genesis 3, this relationship also became a casualty of the fall. When confronted with his sin, Adam blamed Eve for his failure. The principle for Christian community development is that our efforts have to build up the family unit if we envision our communities as places where we are to experience some of God's provisions in Paradise.[128]

Thus, this seems to imply that Christian community development hinges on our relationship with God. The Bible says that these new believers had all things in *common*. The Holy Spirit had changed their perspective about mammon and materials. They began to share with another as a radical community of followers of Christ. They spent their time and their resources on what would benefit the whole, not just individual members of individual

---
[127] Franklin, *Another Day's Journey*, 31.
[128] Phil Reed, "Toward a Theology of Christian Community Development," in Perkins, *Restoring At-Risk Communities*, 29.

families. They were to become a family of families, sharing their resources for the health and well-being of all.

In contemporary Western society, there is too much pressure to acquire possessions, protect possessions, maintain possessions, and insure possessions. We need to reinvest in our communities. The money in the African American community does not circulate more than once. We spend our money outside of the very communities that need our money. As we reassess our priorities, we should privilege the objective of lifting the lot of the least of these. We can only do that by radically redistributing our resources. As Reed points out:

> Redistribution means providing opportunities to the poor to obtain the skills and economic resources to be able to work their way out of poverty, whatever the cause for their situation. Redistribution means putting our lives, our skills, our education, and our resources to work to empower the people in a community of need…redistribution is not complete until the community has its own economic base.
>
> On redistribution, we want to make it clear that we are not talking about the seizing of someone's property. Redistribution is not socialism or communism. We are making the case that when God is working in the hearts of his people they will want to use his resources in accordance with his principles. One of the clear principles in Scripture is God's concern for economic development of the poor.[129]

The Acts Two Community witnessed the establishment of new partnerships among this diverse group of people. They "heard each in their own language." This is a signal that God was breaking down barriers between ethnic groups, and class, and gender. As mutual beings we are establish relationships and alliances that edify the body and bring the greatest good to the society. The reallocation of resources will require new partnerships. Paternalism is a negative action in social service. We should not help others because we believe that we are better than them and we are the only ones who can help them. True service is motivated by genuine love and respect for others. We give priority to those who need it most, but we also recognize that we are recipients of amazing grace and abundant mercy. Our proper response is to help others and establish new relationships that are mutually edifying

---
[129] Ibid., 34-35.

and empowering. We then become business partners – in the business of community building. John Perkins talks about economic development as a necessary aspect of community development:

> Economic development then becomes asset management. Asset management finally grows into developing an enterprise that you own. The challenge for Christian community-based economic development, then, is to enable the people of the community to start local enterprises that meet local needs and employ indigenous people.[130]

In Acts three, which immediately follows the Acts two community fellowship, partnership is re-established. Peter and John had competed for the affection and favor of Jesus Christ before his death. They were both a part of Jesus' inner circle. John wants to be "the disciple whom Jesus loved."[131] Peter is the disciple for whom Jesus sends after his resurrection. The disciples were wary of Peter after he denied Jesus at the most critical period of his life. Something changes on the Day of Pentecost. The Holy Spirit ushers forth a new family of followers. The leadership exhibits a new model of service based on Jesus' teachings. Peter and John bury their hatchet and re-establish their partnership because they were empowered by the Holy Ghost. They were no longer in competition, but in collaboration. They were no longer jockeying for position, but they were joined in purpose. African Americans have to be committed to building new partnerships between the religious, civic, academic and business communities. We must be committed to partnering across demographic boundaries. The Holy Spirit is clearly the most important agent of revitalization of community which must not be relegated to the four walls of the church building, but must be unleashed into the community to bring the dry bones to life and the rebuilding of the old waste places. Franklin notes:

> Perhaps the most remarkable development in black church culture during the post-civil rights era has been its spiritual renewal through the expanding influence of the least familiar forms of black church tradition, namely, Afro-Pentecostal churches and leaders. This is all the more remarkable because this segment of the black church community has not simply been ignored by most church scholars and leaders but has long

---
130   Ibid., 43.
131   John 21:7 & 20.

been a source of scorn and suspicion by mainline American churches and by the assimilated black affluent class. Indeed, during the 1970s and '80s, there were significant denominational culture wars over how contemporary Christians should regard this segment of the church and its claims about the person and work of the Holy Spirit. Riverside Church (former) pastor Dr. James Forbes regarded this skirmish as the American church's opportunity to rediscover and redeem the Third Person of the Trinity in their theologies and liturgical lives..[132]

After being empowered by the Holy Spirit, Peter and John, leaders in the new community, go to the temple with a new sense of urgency. They are going to worship and witness. Ironically, they are met by a lame man at a gate called beautiful. There is a test for the leaders of the new community. They had shared what they had with each other. Now they were challenged by someone outside of their community. The man is relegated to begging for help because of his condition. He cannot work to support himself. All he can do now is ask for a handout. Peter and John insisted on setting the terms for a new partnership by telling the man, "Look at us." This was the first time the man was encountered as a full human being rather than a problem. They wanted the *lame* man to be known as a *real* man. His condition did not disqualify him from a membership in a new community. They told the man, "Silver and gold we do not have...." They said this not because they didn't want to share with him as they had just done with others. They said this because they had more than money to give him.

Our communities need more resources, more money, more businesses, better jobs, better housing, and better schools. We have the power to improve our communities. But money alone is not the answer. We need to declare to broken, hurting, lame people, "In the Name of Jesus of Nazareth, rise up and walk!" We no longer see them as people with problems, but people with potential. We can see them as rich resources and abundant assets. John Kretzmann and John McKnight talk about the need for an asset-based model of community development that begins with the assets instead of the deficits of a community:

---

[132] Franklin, *Crisis in the Village*, 167-68.

Each community boasts a unique combination of assets upon which to build its future. A thorough map of those assets would begin with an inventory of the gifts, skills and capacities of the community's residents. Household by household, building by building, block by block, the capacity mapmakers will discover a vast and often surprising array of individual talents and productive skills, few of which are being mobilized for community-building purposes... It is essential to recognize the capacities, for example, of those who have been labeled mentally handicapped or disabled, or of those who are marginalized because they are too old, or too young, or too poor. In a community whose assets are being fully recognized and mobilized, these people too well will be part of the action, not as clients or recipients of aid, but as full contributors to the community-building process.[133]

The Black Church has always excelled when it has been able to leverage resources by "stepping out on faith." The Black Church has built phenomenal ministries and prodigious edifices on the foundation of hope. Potential is realized when possibilities are pursued. We may not have had much "silver and gold," but what we have had has been more than enough. The spirit of *umoja* and *ujamaa*, the power of *kujichagulia* and *kuumba*, the capacity of *nia* and *umoja*, and the everlasting hope of *imani* has sustained and propelled the Black Church in America forward for four centuries. Sharing the greatest resource we have, our collective faith, will help to restore and rebuild our communities with more than brick and mortar. We've come this far by faith.

---

133 John P. Kretzmann and John L. McKnight, *Building Communities from the Inside Out: A Path Toward Finding and Mobilizing a Community's Assets*, (Chicago: ACTA Publications, 1993), 6.

APPENDIX A:
BIBLE STUDY DISCUSSION GUIDE FOR AN AFRICENTRIC MINISTRY APPROACH FOR PROPHETIC COMMUNITY ENGAGEMENT

INTRODUCTION

The praxis model for empowering the congregation to do prophetic engagement can be described in five parts: 1. Our mandate; 2. Our mission; 3. Our mindset; 4. Our ministry; 5. Our mutuality. These five parts can be correlated to the seven principles (Nguzu Saba) of Kwanzaa: Umoja, Ujima, Kuumba, Kujichagulia, Nia, Imani, Ujamaa and Imani.

One of the keys to restoring African American communities is an indigenous cultural and spiritual reconnection with the Black Church, and vice versa. In order for the connection to be authentic, it has to be more than transactional – political or economic. The connection has to be anchored in the recovery of a "holy common ground." At the center of this "holy common ground" is a truly African spiritual ethos. While many churches have made the overt attempt to infuse Africentrism (to be defined later), most have been drawn to the current evangelical trends that tend to "de-culturalize" and "de-colorize" the Gospel. There appears to be a direct correlation between racial/social integration and the "de-radicalization" of the Black Church, which Gayraud Wilmore refers to as "the process of lessening social and political advocacy of Black ministers and churches in urban areas."[134]

The specific goal of this work is redress the economic injustice experienced in a poor African American community – the Upton Community – by pursuing a holistic strategy of community development. This is best achieved by empowering people to become self-sufficient through the power of the Gospel. One of the most prolific and effective proponents of Christian (Church-based) Community Development is Rev. John Perkins. Rev. Perkins presents three principles for authentic, grassroots, Christian community development: 1. Relocation: To minister effectively to the poor one must relocate in the

---
134 Gayraud Wilmore, *Black Religion and Black Radicalism*, (Maryknoll, NY: Orbis Books, 2000).

community of need. Jesus identified with people's felt need where they were. 2. Reconciliation: The gospel has the power to reconcile people both to God and to each other. Reconciliation is not an optional aspect of the Gospel. Jesus constantly overcame racial, religious, gender barriers. 3. Redistribution: Christ calls us to share with those in need, redistributing more than our goods.

PART ONE: OUR MANDATE – EZEKIEL 37

Our Mandate: Umoja (Unity): Our mandate is to seek and maintain unity that begins with our relationship with God, affirms our connection to Africa and the Diaspora, and calls forth solidarity among and liberation for all of God's people.

Thesis: The key to transforming our Communities (Dry Bones) is a life-transforming experience with the Holy Spirit. That Spirit in turn will lead us to speak a Word of New Life. Although it looks dire, drear, and dry we still have an obligation to say something to the bones. Relevant Proclamation is contingent upon proximity and sensitivity, which leads to receptivity and connectivity.

God sensitizes the prophet by sending him to the Valley. He doesn't do it to peak his curiosity but to raise his conscience. You don't have anything to SAY if you haven't had anything to SEE. I am not sure if you realized it lately, but we are in the Valley.

Dr. King's quote: "Any religion that professes to be concerned about the soul, but is unconcerned about the conditions that damage the soul is a dry-as-dust religion."

In this text we can discern three types of Dry Bones:
1. **Dead – Spiritually Lifeless; Soulless**
2. **Despondent and Dejected:** They have suffered so much loss. Their community has been systemically underdeveloped and disenfranchised for so long that they've given up hope of ever being revived. They have become hopeless because of the continual systemic economic injustice: inferior services, schools, and resources.
3. **Disassembled and Dispersed:** They have been torn asunder as a community. Their families have deteriorated. Their kinship ties

are dwindling. Their neighborly ties are diminishing. They are disconnected from each other, from God, from community and the Church. Isolation and separation has become normal.

As the Church of Jesus Christ, and as proclaimers of the Gospel, the Good News, God is calling us to say something. I would like to suggest to you there are THREE interrelated ways that we can say something, based on the experience of the prophet Ezekiel.

STRATEGY

1. **REVIEW THE SETTING (PASTORAL):** Verses 1-3
   a. A Strategic Plan begins with care and sensitivity to the context
   b. God began with moving (physically and spiritually) the "Pastor"
   c. A word of encouragement
   d. We are Shepherds and not hirelings (read Ezekiel 34:11-16)
   e. Dwight L. Moody once said, "There are a good many lean sheep in God's fold, but not in his pasture."
   f. We have to say something because we have a PASTORAL OBLIGATION

2. **RESPOND TO THE SITUATION (PRIESTLY):** Verse 4-8
   a. Stop Judging the Bones ("These bones probably got what they deserved.")
   b. Stop stigmatizing and marginalizing the Bones ("They belong in the Valley.")
   c. Stop Paternalizing the Bones ("You bones sure are sorry. You need me to help me you.")
   d. Speak to the Bones
   e. Healing – restoration and regeneration (verse 5-6)
   f. A ministry of encouragement
   g. We have to say something because we have a PRIESTLY OBLIGATION

2. **RESTATE THE SOLUTION (PROPHETIC):** Verses 9-10
   a. Engage the powers that be. Do not be disengaged and disconnected from the living reality of the people and the forces that afflict our people.

b. We have to say something because we have a PROPHETIC OBLIGATION
c. The Bones had form, but did not have power
d. The Problem is our dry bones have aggregated and assimilated, but have not activated
e. If our dry bones could ever connect with the community's dry bones, we could be a great army.

QUESTIONS FOR REFLECTION:

- Think about and discuss ways that our congregation can use Bible study centered on the Jewish experience of exile, disconnectedness and dispersion to open the way for deeper understanding about what it means to be an African in Diaspora and a Black Christian in Baltimore.
- Discuss and create a plan for a series of church-wide studies (for adults, youth and children) on specific places in the Diaspora, the United States and greater Baltimore that will create a greater awareness of our congregation's Unity and a stronger commitment to working with others for liberation and empowerment.
- Find persons in the congregation who were raised or lived in the Upton Community. Invite them to share their own personal experiences and help the congregation as it explores the historical, geographical, political and cultural background of this community in relation to other communities.

PART TWO: OUR MISSION – ISAIAH 58

Our Mission: *Ujima* (Collective work/Responsibility) and *Kuumba* (Creativity): Our mission is to build and maintain our communities as Africans in Diaspora who live in a context of service and mutual accountability in America and the world, strengthened by the liberation spirit of God (*Ujima*); and to ground our creative energy in a renewed and renewing relationship with God that restores our African American communities and creates new possibilities for commitment to the Diaspora and the world for the benefit of all people (*Kuumba*).

Today like 8th Century Israelites we are facing the challenge of our era. We cannot see our future without facing our past. The space we occupy is on the axis of a spinning tower that is viewing the remnants of a once stable and desirable neighborhood. What has happened in our community, to our people, is objectionable and abhorrent. We are like exiles returning to our own land but not recognizing where we are. The landscape has been scorched and the horizon has been ransacked. What was a "promised land" in the great Black migration of the 20th century has become a "wasteland" in the so-called "post-racial" 21st century.

Thesis: There is a major divide between the Black Church and African American Community. We need to construct a bridge that reconnects the Church and the Community into one unified yet diverse whole. The mission of transforming African American communities in inner cities must involve recapturing our African spirituality in a contemporary context. This is a two-fold venture. On the one-hand it involves *reconciling* the rupturing relationship between the Black Church and the Black community. On the other hand it involves *restoring* a sense of "communality" that is central to African and African American identity. Reconciliation must first involve acknowledgement of a fault and/or violation of the relationship before forgiveness and resolution can occur. In this sense the Black Church can be prophetic in calling out the "sin" of its own negligence and apathy toward the suffering of the Black Community. The Black Church can also be priestly in bringing about healing and reconciliation by extending compassion and concern for the well-being of the victimized and the vulnerable. Rebuilding, Repairing and Restoring are CREATIVE (Kuumba) acts of the Church.

Chapter 58 is a call for a true fast: Reconciliation

STRATEGY

1. **REBUILD THE CHURCH (SPIRITUAL) (Build the old waste places)**
    a. **You know it's hard to see the need for remodeling in your own home when you stay in it all the time. You get used to disorder and disrepair.**
    b. Isaiah says God's first issue is with the Church. While we're spending so much time passing judgment on the world, we need to see the mote in our own eye.
    c. We must take this unique opportunity to reevaluate our relationship with God and our job performance as it relates to our mission.

d. Bishop Walter Scott Thomas really challenged me when he asked the question, "Is there anything going on in your church today that is worth Jesus dying for?"
   e. Confess our sins, repent, seek forgiveness and reconciliation.
   f. I know charity begins at home, but so does judgment.
   g. The answer to rebuilding is found in verses 6-9
      i. The church has almost become a spiritual waste place – the remains of once great movement.
      ii. But thank God, there is still a foundation to build on!
   h. Jesus said, "Upon this rock I will build my Church and the gates of hell shall not prevail against it." Hell is knocking on the doors of the Church. And maybe some doors need to be knocked in. And maybe some walls need to be broken down. But that's alright, 'cause we've got a firm foundation. "On Christ the solid rock I stand…"

2. **REPAIR THE CHASM (Repairer of the Breach)**
   a. There has been a major break, a violation, an egregious error
   b. There is a rift in our relationship between the Church and the Community; a separation that is spiritual, cultural and moral.

POEM: THE BRIDGE BUILDER

An old man, going a lone highway,
Came, at the evening, cold and gray,
To a chasm, vast, and deep, and wide,
Through which was flowing a sullen tide.

The old man crossed in the twilight dim;
The sullen stream had no fear for him;
But he turned, when safe on the other side,
And built a bridge to span the tide.

"Old man," said a fellow pilgrim, near,
"You are wasting strength with building here;
Your journey will end with the ending day;
You never again will pass this way;
You've crossed the chasm, deep and wide-
Why build you this bridge at the evening tide?"

The builder lifted his old gray head:
"Good friend, in the path I have come," he said,
"There followeth after me today,
A youth, whose feet must pass this way.

This chasm, that has been naught to me,
To that fair-haired youth may a pitfall be.
He, too, must cross in the twilight dim;
Good friend, I am building this bridge for him."

   c. We must be bridge-builders

3. **RESTORE THE COMMUNITY (SOCIAL)**
   (The Restorer of Streets to Dwell in)
   a. The Message translation says: You'll be known as those who can fix anything, restore old ruins, rebuild and renovate, make the community livable again.
   a. We should be known as restorers. This is the year of recovery.
   a. What does a restored community look like? (Harlem Children's Zone)
   a. What does Zion mean?

"**If my people who are called by my name will humble themselves and pray…**" **2 Chronicles 7:14**

"**How to reach the masses men of every birth; for an answer, Jesus gave the Key…**"

He said, If I, If I be lifted up from the earth, I'll draw all men unto me
O the world is hungry for the living bread…
Lift Him up. Lift Him up. Still he speaks from eternity…

QUESTIONS FOR REFLECTION:

- What are some of the ways that our congregation has experienced Collective Work/Responsibility? What are some ways we can experience that in our broader community or neighborhood?
- Think of ways that collective efforts in our congregation's ministries have been difficult? What do you think are the sources of these difficulties and how can they be addressed?

- What are some ways that we can work in more collective and responsible partnership with each other and with our community?
- What are some of the areas in our congregational life where restoration and revitalization are needed? What are some of the barriers preventing these changes and how they can be addressed?
- What are some of the areas in our community where our congregation can become a "repairer of the breach?"
- What new levels of faith commitment are required, both individually and collectively, for such a change and how can they be supported and sustained?

PART THREE: OUR MINDSET – NEHEMIAH 4:1-20

Our Mindset: Kujichagulia (Self-Determination): Our mindset is to define ourselves as daughters and sons of Africa in America, created in the image of God, and willing to participate in the liberation of those in the Diaspora and the world.

Thesis: Our community has suffered because we have turned a jaundice eye and a deaf ear to the plight of our land. It has become "out of sight, out of mind." Nehemiah was the catalyst for the change, the leader of the movement and the spokesman for the nation, but the wall was rebuilt and the community was transformed because the people had a mind to work. We need some Nehemiah's who have succeeded, gotten education, who have access to resources – financial and human – who will be sensitized to the plight of our community. We need some Nehemiahs who will not just pray and pontificate, but who will prophesy and testify, worship and work, fast and fight, to rebuild the walls of this community.

POEM: A BUILDER OR A WRECKER?

As I watched them tear a building down
A gang of men in a busy town
With a ho-heave-ho, and a lusty yell
They swung a beam and the side wall fell

I asked the foreman, "Are these men skilled,
And the men you'd hire if you wanted to build?"

He gave a laugh and said, "No, indeed,
Just common labor is all I need."

"I can easily wreck in a day or two,
What builders have taken years to do."
And I thought to myself, as I went my way
Which of these roles have I tried to play?

Am I a builder who works with care,
Measuring life by rule and square?
Am I shaping my work to a well-made plan
Patiently doing the best I can?

Or am I a wrecker who walks to town
Content with the labor of tearing down?
"O Lord let my life and my labors be
That which will build for eternity!"

The Profile of the Kinds of Opposition faced by Builders
Blockers
Wreckers
Fence-sitters

"When evil men plot, good men must plan. When evil men burn and bomb, good men must build and bind. When evil men shout ugly words of hatred, good men must commit themselves to the glories of love." Dr. Martin Luther King, Jr.

THREE POINTS:

1. **Internal Fortitude**
    a. Spiritual Strength
    b. Emotional Maturity
    c. Moral Responsibility
    d. A Mighty Fortress is Our God
    e. No other foundation can any man lay, except that which is laid…

2. **External Focus**
    a. The Church is suffering from "navel-gazing," looking at ourselves

    b. You cannot be obsessed with the obvious. You cannot be confused by the concession.
    c. You need some folk who will be camped on the wall looking at what on the outside. We need some folk who are circumference on the camp
    d. We need some folk who can do a socio-political critique of the condition of the community

3. Eternal Favor
    a. Nehemiah had favor with another King
    b. Nehemiah was resourceful because of his connection to the King
    c. Nehemiah's earthly favor was coupled with the heavenly, eternal favor of the King of Kings
    d. When you have favor of the King you can say, "I'm doing a great work and I can't come down!" That gains more favor with the King.

PART FOUR: OUR MINISTRY – LUKE 4:16-22

Our Ministry: Nia (Purpose): Our ministry is to build and develop our communities in ways that acknowledge the sacredness of our collective work of liberation in the Diaspora and the world and our dependence on God's power and grace to perform it.

    I am seeing the 4th Chapter of Luke this week with fresh eyes. I've seen something in the text that I've never seen before. The chapter begins with the temptation of Jesus in the wilderness and ends with the first threat on Jesus' life after His prophetic proclamation of His mission to preach good news to the poor. What I saw encapsulated in this chapter for the first time is that before you can accept your mission and fulfill your mission to do ministry on holy common ground in the community and in the world you've got to deal with your demons on two fronts: your personal demons and your religious demons.

    My good friend Dr. Raphael Warnock, the pastor of Ebenezer Baptist Church of Atlanta, and former pastor of Douglas Community Church here in Baltimore, helped me this week at the Morehouse preaching festival when he dealt with the first part of Luke 4.[135] You have to resist three carnal impulses. You see before he could begin his ministry, Christ had to deal with Jesus. You

---
[135] Rev. Dr. Raphael G. Warnock. Sermon preached at Martin Luther King, Jr. Chapel, Morehouse College, April 4, 2011.

make think this homiletical heresy or theological blasphemy, but I just believe that the Savior had to deal with him self before he could save others.

Resist the narrow impulse to self-service. (Turn stones into bread) When Jesus makes bread it isn't for himself. The temptation is to make *A (one)* loaf of bread. Jesus is concerned with the multitude.

Resist the narcissistic impulse to self-aggrandizement. (Bow down and worship the devil and all this will be yours.) It can never be about you. Don't make a deal with the devil just to get what you want. The glory goes to God, not to self. "Get behind me Satan!"

Resist the non-sensical impulse to self-destruction. (Throw yourself down from the pinnacle of the temple). You're better off dealing with the demons while you're on the ground. In order, to do ministry on holy common ground you've got to get over yourself.

The second half of the chapter is the answer to the devilish and demonic tendencies of carnal people (Beginning with verses 16-18)

1. **Receive A Priestly Call:** "The Spirit of the Lord is upon me, because he has anointed me to preach Good News to the poor." The anointing is a sign of God's blessing, power and authority. It is not a call to domination or superiority. It is a call to service. It flows from the head to keep you from getting full of yourself. And flows to the feet to keep you humble and remind you to serve.
2. **Reveal A Prophetic Claim:** (verses 18-19) This was radical stuff. He identified the victims and the vulnerable. His concern was not for pity and sympathy but for empowerment and liberation. (The New Jim Crow) This was about systems and powers, not about programs.
3. **Report A Personal Conviction:** (verses 20-22) He read the Scripture and he closed the book. He was no longer repeating what was in the book. He stated what was in His heart.
4. **Rebuff A Public Challenge:** (verses 28-30) The people will turn on you when you call them out. Be prepared to deal with opposition and character assassination.

PART FIVE – OUR MUTUALITY (ACTS 2: 41-47)

Our Mutuality: Ujamaa (Cooperative Economics): Our mutuality is the belief in and demonstration of a holistic, multidimensional stewardship that values all of our mutual resources, including material, human, intellectual, and spiritual gifts, as blessings to us from God to be developed and used in African American communities, the Diaspora, and the world for the good of all people.

1. **Reassess** Our Priorities
    a. Spring Inventory
    b. Jesus had taught the Disciples a new code of ethics: Love God with all your heart....and love your NEIGHBOR as you love yourself. Not about retaliation, retribution and recrimination. But it's about reconciliation and restoration.
    c. Three Simple Rules: Do no harm, Do good, Stay in love with God

2. **Reallocate** Our Possessions
    a. They had all things in COMMON. There is too much pressure to acquire possessions, protect possessions, maintain and insure possessions...
    b. We need to reinvest in our communities. The money in the African American community does not circulate more than once.

3. **Re-establish** Our Partnerships
    a. As Mutual Beings we are establish relationships and alliances that edify the body and bring the greatest good to the society
    b. Look at Acts 3: Peter and John bury their hatchet and re-establish their partnership because they were empowered by the Holy Ghost. They were no longer in competition, but in collaboration. They were no longer jockeying for position, but they were joined in purpose.
    c. They told the man, "Silver and gold we do not have...." Not because they didn't want to share. But because they had more than that to give him.
    d. Give a man fish you feed him for a day...

In the name of Jesus Christ of Nazareth, rise up and walk

We need to rebuke the poverty pimps, and stop giving people a handout, but a hand up

Examples: Credit unions, housing coops, food coops, schools, job training, job creation

APPENDIX B
A CONGREGATIONAL QUESTIONNAIRE FOR PROPHETIC COMMUNITY ENGAGEMENT

PRELIMINARY QUESTIONNAIRE[136]

1. The Black Church, especially in urban areas, historically has been an "all-comprehending institution" (Lewis Baldwin), providing an array of human services for residents of the community. Does the Church still have a responsibility for these services? Why or why not?

2. What does the Black Church and the African American community have in common other than racial identity? In your opinion, has the relationship between the two become divided, divorced and/or diminished over the last twenty to thirty years? How so?

3. Many urban areas have been populated by persons that have been described as "the underclass" because of issues such as chronic unemployment and underemployment, substandard education, inferior housing and poor health. The Black Church's leadership, like the Prophet Ezekiel, has had to "speak to dry bones" in desolate and destitute areas that have been underdeveloped and disinvested. Does the Bible or the Church instruct leaders today to address the needs of people in "ghettoes" and underserved communities? If so, how?

4. God commanded the prophet Isaiah in Chapter 58 to tell the people that ritual fasting was not enough because the people were ignoring more important matters of justice, mercy and compassion. He instructed them to "repair the breach and restore the old waste places." In our church how are we seeking to engage the important matters of justice, mercy

---

[136] Adapted in part from, *Urban Churches, Vital Signs*, Nile Harper, Eugene, Oregon: Wipf and Stock Publishers, 1999) and *Living God's Politics: A Guidebook for Putting Your Faith into Action*, Jim Wallis and Chuck Gutenson (New York: HarperCollins, 2006).

and compassion in the city? If we are not, in what ways can we fulfill this commandment?

5. Christians are part of the body of Christ, knit together by the Holy Spirit into a community of worship and witness, within a global community created by God and for which Christ gave himself. How is our church present as Christ's body in the world, doing the work of reconciliation and transformation? What are some specific ways in which our church seeks to be the body of Christ in this neighborhood?

6. We are all children of God, and we are all citizens of the political community. Beyond paying taxes and voting, what does your Christian faith motivate you to do in order to build up the common good of our society?

7. Who owns the businesses, service companies, retail stores, food stores and lending institutions in our community? What degree of local ownership is there in this community? In the church?

8. What does the Bible say about God's concern for the most vulnerable citizens or those on the margins of society? What do you think God's expectations for us are with regard to these concerns (both at the personal and public levels)? What steps would you suggest for the Church and congregation members to begin to live into those expectations?

9. To what extent does the income from goods and services produced in our community get reinvested with the community? Does it largely leave the area as profit for absentee owners who are not invested in the community? Think of specific businesses.

10. To what extent do the people of our community have open access to good quality, affordable housing as owners or renters? Are some groups more able to secure good housing than other groups?

11. What is the attitude and action of the city government toward our community? Who are the city council and state representatives from this

area? What is the quality of the relationship between the state government and this community?

12. What is your own attitude toward and involvement with local and state government in relation to this community? Can you think of some ways in which the church has affected how you think and act in relation to local government?

13. How do issues of crime, safety, police protection and community participation in local street safety affect this community?

14. Over the past decade what significant changes have taken place in this community that affect the quality of life and levels of opportunity?

15. What major losses have taken place in this community that tend to create inequity, insecurity, and a sense of injustice? To what extent has the church responded to these losses?

16. Are there significant ethnic, racial religious or social conflicts in the community? To what extent are these openly recognized? Are these conflicts related to the operation of public and other institutions in this community?

17. What are the physical assets within this community – for example, parks, schools, open land, commercial buildings, hospitals, colleges, sports facilities, church buildings, community centers, shopping centers, and libraries? What are some ways in which some of these assets might be resources for helping to solve some of the challenges facing our community?

18. What human resources are in this community? Who are some key leaders, talented and skilled people, persons with special experience, long-time residents who know the community's history, younger persons with energy, middle-aged persons with useful connections, political figures, clergy, local business owners, school principals and teachers, leaders of voluntary organizations and service clubs? Make a list of five or six persons in the community who might be helpful in engaging the challenges facing this area.

19. What are some of the service and information resources within this community – for example, school librarians, city librarians, city government agencies, social welfare agencies, police department, fire department, college faculty and research institutes, federal census reports, city planning documents, clergy, regional planning bodies, computer internet, local and regional newspapers? To what extent has the Church used these information resources to promote adult education, mission planning, and thinking about assets?

20. What potential partnerships, locally or regionally, might our Church be able to create in the Greater Baltimore metropolitan area? Who might have knowledge, skill, experience, financial assets, political connections, and a willingness to join with us in doing new things to meet human needs? Make a list of five or six such persons or institutions where such persons might be found.

21. What foundations, corporations, government agencies, and other voluntary organizations can you identify that could be invited to become partners in working for positive change and greater social justice? Make a list of five to ten such potential partners.

BIBLIOGRAPHY

Andrews, Dale P. *Practical Theology for Black Churches*, Louisville: Westminster John Knox Press, 2002.

Asante, Molefi Kete. *Afrocentricity: The Theory of Social Change (Revised and Expanded)*. Chicago: African American Images, 2003.

_____, *The Afrocentric Idea*. Philadelphia, PA: Temple University Press, 1998.

Ashby, Homer U.. *Our Home is Over Jordan: A Black Pastoral Theology*. St. Louis: Chalice Press, 2003.

Block, Peter. *Community: The Structure of Belonging*. San Francisco: Berrett-Koehler Publishers, 2009.

Bruggeman, Walter. *The Prophetic Imagination*, 2nd ed. Minneapolis: Fortress Press, 2001.

Butler, Jr., Lee H. *Liberating Our Dignity, Saving Our Souls*. St. Louis: Chalice Press, 2006.

_____. *A Loving Home: Caring for African American Marriage and Families*. Cleveland: Pilgrim Press, 2000.

Chinula, Donald M. *Building King's Beloved Community: Foundations for Pastoral Care and Counseling with the Oppressed*. Cleveland, OH: United Church Press, 1997.

Cone, James H., *For My People: Black Theology and the Black Church*. Maryknoll, NY: Orbis Books, 2000.

_____. *A Black Theology of Liberation*, 2nd ed. Maryknoll, NY: Orbis Books, 2002.

Conn, Harvie M. and Ortiz, Manuel. *Urban Ministry: The Kingdom, the City and the People of God*. Downers Grove, IL: InterVarsity Press, 2001.

Donaldson, Dave and Carlson-Thies, Stanley, *A Revolution of Compassion: Faith-Based Groups as Full Partners in Fighting America's Social Problems*. Grand Rapids: Baker Books, 2003.

Evans, Jr., James H. *We Shall All Be Changed: Social Problems and Theological Renewal.* Minneapolis: Fortress Press, 1997.

_____. *We Have Been Believers: An African American Systematic Theology.* Minneapolis: Fortress Press, 1992.

Felton, Carroll M., Jr.. *The Care of Souls in the Black Church: A Liberation Perspective.* New York: Martin Luther King Fellows Press, 1980.

Flake, Floyd H., Flake, Elaine McCollins, and Edwin C. Reed. *African American Church Management Book.* Valley Forge: Judson Press, 2005.

Franklin, Robert M. *Another Day's Journey: Black Churches Confronting the American Crisis.* Minneapolis: Fortress Press, 1997

_____, *Crisis in the Village: Restoring Hope in African American Communities.* Minneapolis: Fortress Press, 2007.

Freire, Paulo, *Pedagogy of the Oppressed.* New York: Continuum, 1999.

Gutierrez, Gustavo., *A Theology of Liberation.* Maryknoll, NY: Orbis Books, 1988.

Harper, Nile. *Urban Churches, Vital Signs: Beyond Charity Towards Justice.* Eugene, OR: Wipf & Stock, 1999.

Harris, Sr., Forest E. *Ministry for Social Crisis: Theology and Praxis in the Black Church Tradition.* Macon, GA: Mercer University Press, 1993.

_____, Roberson, James T., and George, Larry D. *What Does it Mean to be Black and Christian?* Nashville: Townsend Press, 1995

Harris, James H. *Pastoral Theology: A Black-Church Perspective.* Minneapolis: Fortress Press, 1991.

_____, *Preaching Liberation.* Minneapolis: Fortress Press, 1995.

Harrison, Roland Kenneth. *Introduction to the Old Testament.* Peobody, Massachusetts: Prince Press, 1999.

Hicks, Ivan Douglas. *Centering African American Religion: Toward an Afrocentric Analysis*, A Doctoral Dissertation submitted to Temple University, Ann Arbor, MI: UMI Dissertation Services, 2003

Hilliard, Asa G., "Liberating the Ancient Utterances," in Carruthers, Iva E., Haynes, Frederick D., II, Wright, Jr., Jeremiah A., *Blow the Trumpet in Zion: Global Vision and Action for the 21st Century Black Church.* Philadelphia: Fortress Press, 2005

Ivory, Luther D., *Toward a Theology of Radical Involvement: The Theological Legacy of Martin Luther King Jr.,* Nashville: Abingdon Press, 1997.

Jacobsen, Dennis A. *Doing Justice: Congregations and Community Organizing.* Minneapolis: Fortress Press, 2001.

Jennings, Theodore W. *Good News to the Poor: John Wesley's Evangelical Economics.* Nashville: Abingdon, 1990.

Kretzmann, John P. and John L. McKnight. *Building Communities from the Inside Out.* Chicago: ACTA Publications, 1993.

Lartey, Emmanuel Y.. *In Living Colour: An Intercultural Approach to Pastoral Care and Counseling.* Herndon, VA: Cassell Publishers, 1997.

Lincoln, C. Eric and Lawrence Mamiya. *The Black Church in the African American Experience.* Durham and London: Duke University Press, 1990.

Linthicum, Robert C., *Empowering the Poor: Community Organizing among the City's "Rag, Tag and Bobtail."* Monrovia, CA: MARC/World Vision, 1991.

Lupton, Robert D., *Renewing the City: Reflections on Community Development and Urban Renewal*, Downers Grove, IL: InterVarsity Press, 2005.

Malone, Walter, Jr. *The Black Church and Community Economic Empowerment through a Community Development Corporation*, (Unpublished D.Min. thesis, United Theological Seminary, Dayton, Ohio), 1993.

_____. *From Holy Power to Holy Profits: The Black Church and Community Economic Empowerment.* Chicago: African American Images, 1994.

Marsh, Charles. *The Beloved Community: How Faith Shapes Social Justice, From the Civil Rights Movement to Today.* New York: Basic Books, 2005.

Mbiti, John S. *African Religions and Philosophy*, 2nd ed. Portsmouth, NH: Heineman Publishers, 1999.

McDougall, Harold. *Black Baltimore: A New Theory of Community.* Philadelphia: Temple University Press, 1993.

McKnight, John and Peter Block. *The Abundant Community: Awakening the Power of Families and Neighborhoods.* San Francisco: Berrett-Koehler Publishers, 2010.

McMickle, Marvin A., *Where Have All the Prophets Gone?: Reclaiming Prophetic Preaching in America.* Cleveland: Pilgrim Press, 2006.

Orr, Marion. *Black Social Capital: The Politics of School Reform in Baltimore, 1986-1998.* Lawrence, KS: University of Kansas Press, 1999.

Paris, Peter J. *The Spirituality of African Peoples: The Search for a Common Moral Discourse.* Minneapolis: Fortress Press, 1995.

Pietila, Antero. *Not in My Neighborhood: How Bigotry Shaped a Great American City*. Chicago: Ivan R. Dee, 2010.

Perkins, John. *With Justice for All: A Strategy for Community Development*. Ventura, CA: Regal Books, 2007.

_____, ed, *Restoring At-Risk Communities: Doing It Together & Doing It Right*. Grand Rapids: Baker Books, 1995.

Pinn, Anthony B.. *The Black Church in the Post-Civil Rights Era*. Maryknoll, New York: Orbis Books, 2002.

Proctor, Dennis V.. *A Strategy for Recovering the Liberation Motif of the African Methodist Episcopal Zion Church*. (Unpublished D.Min. Thesis, United Theological Seminary, Dayton, Ohio), 1993.

Roberts, J. Deotis. *Africentric Christianity: A Theological Appraisal for Ministry*. Valley Forge: Judson Press, 2000.

_____. *The Prophethood of Black Believers: An African American Political Theology for Ministry*. Louisville: Westminster John Knox Press, 1994.

_____. *Liberation and Reconciliation: A Black Theology*. Maryknoll: NY, 1994.

Raser, Stephen C. and Micheal J.N. Dash. *The Mark of Zion: Congregational Life in Black Churches*. Cleveland, Ohio: Pilgrim Press, 2003.

Robinson, Eugene. *Disintegration: The Splintering of Black America*, New York: Doubleday, 2010.

Smith Jr., Archie. *Navigating the Deep River: Spirituality in African American Families*. Cleveland: United Church Press, 1997.

Smith, R. Drew, ed. *A New Day Begun: African American Churches and Civic Culture in Post-Civil Rights America*. Durham and London: Duke University Press, 2003.

_____. *Long March Ahead: African American Churches and Public Policy in Post-Civil Rights America*. Durham and London: Duke University Press, 2004.

Speller, Julia. *Walkin' the Talk: Keepin' the Faith in Africentric Congregations*. Cleveland: Pilgrim Press, 2005.

Stewart III, Carlyle Fielding. *Black Spirituality and Black Consciousness*. Trenton, NJ: Africa World Press, 1999.

Taylor, Edward L.. *The Words of Gardner Taylor, Volume 5*. Valley Forge: Judson Press, 2001.

Upton Planning Committee, *Upton Master Plan*, 2004.

Walker, Jr., Theodore. *Empower the People: Social Ethics for the African American Church.* San Jose: Authors Choice Press, 2001.

Wallis, John. *God's Politics: Why the Right Gets it Wrong and the Left Doesn't Get I.*, New York: Harper-Collins Publishers, 2005.

Wallis John and Chuck Gutenson. *Living God's Politics.* New York: Harper-Collins Publishers, 2006.

Washington, Preston. *God's Transforming Spirit.* Maryknoll, New York: Orbis Books, 1990.

Watkins-Ali, Carroll A. *Survival and Liberation: Pastoral Theology in African American Context*, St. Louis: Chalice Press, 1999.

Wilmore, Gayraud. *Pragmatic Spirituality: The Christian Faith through an Africentric Lens.* New York and London: New York University Press, 2004.

_____. *Black Religion and Black Radicalism: An Interpretation of the Religious History of African Americans.* 3rd ed. NY: New York University Press, 2000.

Wimberly, Edward P.. *African American Pastoral Care and Counseling: The Politics of Oppression and Empowerment.* Cleveland: Pilgrim Press, 2006.

Stepping stones